New Tastes of Iowa

A Collection of Lighter, Leaner, Lowered-Fat Recipes from America's Heartland

by Peg Hein

Illustrated by Kathryn Lewis

Copyright© 1993 By Kathryn Designs
All Rights Reserved

No part of this book may be reproduced in any form or by any means without permission from Kathryn Designs.

Edited by Mary Ullrich

ISBN: 0-9613881-2-9

Introduction

There have been a lot of changes in the way people cooked since my first cookbook, **Recipes from Iowa...with Love,** was first printed twelve years ago. Most of those recipes no longer fit the way we now eat. Cooking changed for us when my husband had an emergency heart bypass. His cardiologist told us that a low-fat diet was essential if he was to live to enjoy the retirement years we were looking forward to. I had been an "if it's made with butter, it's better" cook, and now I needed to study, to test recipes, and to try products that were new to me.

The first thing I did was to buy several "low-fat" cookbooks. I discovered that while the recipes were low in fat most of them were also low in taste. If we were to enjoy cooking and eating again, I needed recipes that were both low-fat and good to eat. During the next two years I learned a lot. More and more of the people we came in contact with were on low-fat diets, and we were soon trading recipes and tips on how to safely enjoy one of life's great pleasures.

The next step was to combine the ideas and recipes I had collected with those of good Iowa cooks in a new cookbook about Iowa food to fit today's lifestyle. We hope you like the book and that it encourages you to eat food with less fat and to enjoy it more.

How Much Fat Should You Be Eating?

If you think low-fat diet information is confusing, you have plenty of company. Most people don't know how many grams of fat they should or should not be eating. The Surgeon General of the United States and the American Heart Association tell us to lower the amount of fat in our diets to 30% of the calories we consume. Many cardiologists and weight-loss diets urge us to try for 20-25%. The Pritikin Program and Dr. Dean Ornish have well-known diets that allow only 10% to be fat calories. Your goal should depend on whether you have a health or weight problem; if so, you should consult with your doctor. For most of us the 30% goal of the American Heart Association is adequate and realistic.

So far we've talked about percentages of fat to calories consumed. Yet all recipes and nutrition labels list grams of fat, so it's obvious there is an important step required to translate the percentage of fat in calories into grams of fat.

Most of us have a good idea of the average range of calories we consume. If not, there are many charts giving a suggested range for your height, body build and sex. The easiest way to figure how many grams of fat would be allowed with a goal of 30% is to estimate your calorie intake, drop the last digit and divide by 3. For example, if you average 2,400 calories a day and are satisfied with your weight, drop the last zero and divide 240 by 3. This would mean that 80 grams of fat per day should be your goal. If your average calorie intake is 1500 per day, drop the last zero, divide 150 by 3 and your goal should be 50 grams of fat per day. If you want to try for 25% of the calories in fat, drop the last digit of your calorie intake and divide by 4.

Next, learn to budget your fat grams just as you budget your income. By knowing which foods have little fat and which ones are loaded, you can make smart and easy choices.

Don't think the emphasis on low-fat diets is just another health fad. Every month new research adds to the mounting evidence that fat is the major culprit in 30% of the health problems of Americans. Also, eating low-fat foods is the safest, most satisfying and most permanent way to lose weight.

Simple Steps to a Leaner Diet

There are some simple ways to lower the fat in your diet. And once you start following them, you'll be surprised how easy it is to change your cooking and eating habits. First, rid yourself of the thought that adopting a low-fat diet means no longer being able to eat food you enjoy. Work into the program gradually by starting with these easy steps.

1. Become aware that there are different types of fat. Saturated fats are found in animal products such as meat and dairy products. Trimming the fat from the meat you buy, cutting the size of your servings, using margarine instead of butter and drinking and cooking with skim or 1% milk are major steps towards healthier eating.
2. Try the new fat-free and low-fat products appearing every week on the shelves of our grocery stores. Low-fat salad dressings, reduced-fat mayonnaise, non-fat sour cream and cream cheese and fat-free soups are now available; and if you try them, you'll find that many are really good. If you sampled low-fat products two or three years ago and didn't like them, test some of the new products. Enormous improvements have been made in their taste recently.
3. Invest in at least one good nonstick skillet. If you use it with cooking spray,

you can brown and sauté foods with little or no oil.

4. Use egg substitutes such as Egg Beaters instead of eggs for most of your cooking and eating. You will find the difference in taste of the finished product is minimal.

5. Learn to read the labels found on most food items. For example, when you see that 3 ounces of tuna packed in oil has 15 grams of fat and the same amount of tuna packed in water has 3 grams of fat, your choice becomes easy.

6. Use cocoa instead of baking chocolate and you can have your cake and not feel guilty, too. One ounce of baking chocolate has 15 grams of fat while one tablespoon of cocoa has less than 2 grams of fat.

7. Don't make a big deal about your low-fat diet if you're invited to a friend's for dinner. Just eat less of rich, high-fat foods and make up for any extra by cutting your fat intake over the next few meals. Keep in mind that it is fat intake over a period of time that is significant.

8. Find a book that gives the fat content of different foods. Discovering that simply removing the skin from a chicken breast reduces the fat by 5 grams makes low-fat cooking easy to understand.

9. Watch for recipes that give you the grams of fat. Try out new recipes that sound good until you find several you really like.

10. Don't start out by trying to go too far too fast unless you are under instructions from your doctor. If you cut the amount of fat you eat in an average day from 100 to 70 grams, you will realize a significant difference. That may even be enough for your weight and activity level. As you become more knowledgeable about fat in the diet, you can determine what your goal should be and take whatever steps are still needed.

Once you've adopted these relatively simple measures, you will be making a real difference in your life. It won't be long before you'll find that food with high-fat content no longer tastes good to you. I promise that you'll feel better, live longer and weigh less - and still enjoy eating.

New Tastes of Iowa

CONTENTS

Appetizers 1

Bread and Breakfasts 11

Soups and Salads 21

Main Events 39

Vegetables and Side Dishes 67

Sweets and Treats 87

House Specialties 107

Index 117

Contributors 122

Appetizers

Appetizers

Appetizers can be a dangerous trap for people trying to control fat intake or calories. Served when we are most hungry, one bite of a salty or spicy delicacy often leads to several; and before we know it our good intentions are scuttled by a scrumptious snack loaded with fat, salt and cholesterol. With the introduction of yogurt cheese, non-fat sour cream and a non-fat cream cheese, some of the old favorites can be revised and enjoyed without guilt. Good cooks have managed to find ways to prepare hors d'oeuvres that taste good and are still good for you.

Black Bean Dip

Black beans have almost no fat or cholesterol and lots of fiber. This recipe makes a tasty low-fat appetizer when served with Skinny Dippers or Pita Crisps.

Yields 2 cups   0 grams of fat per serving

- 1 16-ounce can black beans
- 2 cloves garlic, minced
- 2 green onions, minced
- 2 tablespoons fresh lime juice
- ¼ teaspoon Tabasco sauce
- ¼ teaspoon celery seed
- Salt to taste

1. Drain the beans, reserving juice.
2. Combine all of the ingredients except the salt with 1/4 cup of reserved bean juice and place in a food processor or blender.
3. Process briefly, adding more juice if moisture seems thicker than desired. Continue to process until nearly smooth.
4. Add salt to taste.
5. Refrigerate for several hours before serving.

Appetizers

Pita Crisps

Yields 32 pieces *Trace of fat per serving*

4 8-inch whole-wheat pitas
Butter-flavored cooking spray

¼ teaspoon garlic salt
2 teaspoons Parmesan cheese

1. Split each pita by cutting around the outside edge with scissors and separating the two halves. Coat each piece on both sides with the cooking spray.
2. Stack the halves and cut into pie-shaped wedges.
3. Place the wedges on a cookie sheet and sprinkle with the combined garlic salt and Parmesan cheese.
4. Bake at 250° for 20-25 minutes or until crisp.

Skinny Dippers

Yields 32 pieces *Less than 1 gram of fat per stick*

1 package brown-and-serve bread sticks
½ teaspoon onion salt

½ teaspoon celery salt
½ teaspoon garlic powder
Butter-flavored cooking spray

1. Cut each breadstick lengthwise into eight skinny sticks. Spray each stick with cooking spray.
2. Combine the seasonings; sprinkle evenly over the sticks.
3. Broil in the oven for 3-4 minutes or until golden brown. (Watch carefully and turn sticks so they toast evenly.)

Appetizers

Crab-Stuffed Cherry Tomatoes

Serves 10　　　1.5 grams of fat per serving

- 20 cherry tomatoes
- 3 tablespoons low-fat cottage cheese
- 3 tablespoons Hellmann's Reduced Fat Mayonnaise
- 1 teaspoon minced onion
- 1 clove garlic, minced
- 2 tablespoons minced celery
- 2 teaspoons cream-style prepared horseradish
- ½ pound crabmeat, fresh or canned
- Finely chopped chives for garnish

1. Cut off the top of each tomato, scoop out the pulp and turn tomato upside down to drain.
2. Force the cottage cheese through a coarse sieve using the back of a large spoon.
3. Combine remaining ingredients, except crabmeat and chives, with the cottage cheese in a medium bowl and mix well.
4. Chop the crabmeat and add to the cottage cheese mixture.
5. Spoon into the tomato shells and garnish with finely chopped chives.

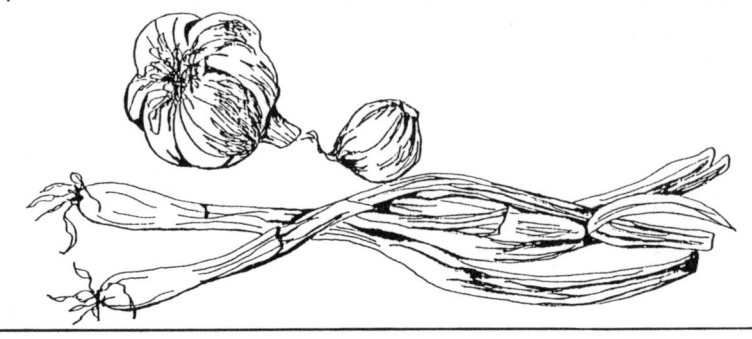

Appetizers

Spinach-Stuffed Mushrooms

Serves 4 *3 grams of fat per serving*

1 pound extra-large mushrooms
Vegetable cooking spray
1 10-ounce box frozen chopped spinach, thawed
3 tablespoons blue cheese fat-free salad dressing
½ cup shredded mozzarella cheese
1 tablespoon egg substitute
¼ teaspoon salt
¼ teaspoon pepper
2 tablespoons bread crumbs
2 teaspoons melted margarine

1. Wipe the mushrooms with a damp paper towel. Remove the stems, mince and reserve.
2. Coat the mushroom caps with the cooking spray and place the caps, stem side up, in a glass baking dish.
3. Squeeze the spinach to remove water, and combine with the chopped mushroom stems.
4. Combine the remaining ingredients, except bread crumbs and margarine, and mix well.
5. Mound the spinach filling into the mushroom caps.
6. Mix the bread crumbs and the margarine and sprinkle lightly over top of the spinach filling.
7. Bake uncovered at 325° for 25 minutes.

Appetizers

Mushroom-Stuffed Shells

These attractive little shells team up with the mushrooms and mozzarella for a winning combination. The shells have no fat and can be used for any savory filling.

Serves 8-10   3.5 grams of fat each

BREAD SHELLS:
24 slices Pepperidge Farm very thin white bread

1. Use a 2½-inch cookie cutter to cut a round from each bread slice. Cut a small pie-shaped wedge from each round.
2. To make the bread flexible, microwave the rounds for 10 seconds on High. Press the rounds into a miniature muffin tin to form a shell.
3. Bake in a preheated 250° oven for 30 minutes or until lightly browned.
4. Fill with whatever filling you choose just before serving.

MUSHROOM FILLING:
Vegetable cooking spray
1 tablespoon margarine
3 green onions, finely chopped
1 clove garlic, minced
½ pound mushrooms, finely chopped

½ cup fresh bread crumbs
½ cup grated mozzarella cheese
Salt and freshly ground pepper

1. Coat a large nonstick skillet with cooking spray. Heat the margarine; add the onions and garlic. Sauté for 2 minutes. Add the mushrooms; cook and stir for another 2 minutes.
2. Mix in the bread crumbs, mozzarella cheese, salt and pepper.
3. Spoon the mushroom mixture into the Bread Shells.
4. Bake in a 350° oven for 10 minutes.

Appetizers

Broiled Shrimp

These tasty shrimp are considered an hors d'oeuvre, but they are also good when served with rice as a main course.

Serves 8   1.4 grams of fat per shrimp

30 fresh or frozen jumbo shrimp
½ cup soy sauce
3 tablespoons oil
¼ cup lemon juice

4 cloves garlic, minced
½ teaspoon black pepper
½ teaspoon freshly ground ginger

1. Thaw the shrimp if frozen. Peel, rinse, drain and pat dry with paper towels.
2. Combine the remaining ingredients in a large bowl.
3. Add the shrimp to the marinade, cover and refrigerate for 1-2 hours. Turn the shrimp occasionally.
4. When ready to cook, remove the shrimp from the marinade.
5. Broil about 6 inches from the broiler element for 1-2 minutes per side, depending on size of shrimp.

♥ When cholesterol was determined to be the cause of the blocking of coronary arteries, a lot of emphasis was placed on lowering the amount of cholesterol in the diet. It is now known that saturated fat causes your body to produce cholesterol and has a greater effect on your cholesterol level than that consumed in your food. Because shrimp has a high-cholesterol count, it was once considered a no-no. Shrimp, with only a trace of fat, is allowed in moderation on a low-fat diet since the new findings.

Appetizers

Iowa Antipasto

Iowans traditionally share special treats with friends and neighbors during the holidays. This tasty, low-fat, low-calorie appetizer is a wonderful antidote to all the rich and fattening foods that go with the season. It is good served as a spread on Pita Crisps.

Yields 6 pints   1.5 grams of fat per 2 tablespoons

- ½ cup olive oil
- 1 medium cauliflower, cut into bite-sized pieces
- 1 large green pepper, chopped
- ½ cup sliced ripe olives
- ½ cup sliced green olives
- 1 cup chopped mushrooms, stems and pieces
- 1 large green pepper, chopped
- 1 cup Heinz HOT catsup
- 1 cup sweeet pickle relish
- 1 cup dill pickle relish
- 1½ cups chunk tuna packed in spring water
- 2 4½-ounce cans peeled tiny shrimp
- 1 cup low-fat Italian salad dressing

1. Combine the oil, cauliflower and green pepper in a large saucepan and simmer for 10 minutes, stirring frequently.
2. Add the olives, mushrooms, HOT catsup and pickle relish. Cook and stir for another 10 minutes.
3. Drain the tuna and shrimp in a large colander and rinse with boiling water. Combine with the mixture in the saucepan.
4. Add the salad dressing and mix gently. Divide the mixture into several jars or containers. Freeze what you will not be using within a few days.

Appetizer

Tortilla Roll-Ups

Yields 4 dozen roll-ups   ½ gram of fat per roll-up

- 1 cup no-fat sour cream
- 1 cup fat-free cream cheese
- 1 4-ounce can chopped green chilies, drained
- 1 4-ounce can chopped ripe olives, drained
- 5 green onions, minced
- 2 cloves garlic, minced
- ½ teaspoon cayenne pepper
- 8 flour tortillas

1. Blend sour cream and cream cheese until smooth.
2. Add the remaining ingredients, except for the tortillas, and mix well.
3. Spread the cheese mixture on the tortillas, roll up and place seam-side down in a glass dish. If the tortillas are not flexible enough to roll easily, cover with paper towels and microwave on High for 10 seconds.
4. Chill for several hours until firm. Slice into ½-inch sections and serve.

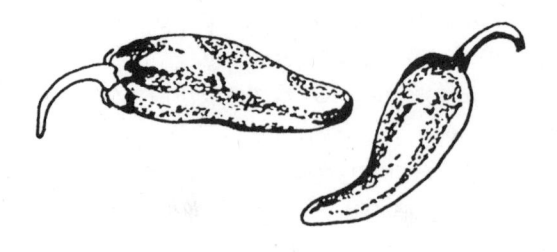

Breads and Breakfasts

Breads and Breakfast

In 1842 Captain Elbridge Gerry Potter journeyed through wild frontier country from St. Louis to St. Paul in search of a site for a farm. He finally settled on 1,400 acres in eastern Iowa near the Mississippi River, naming his farm Paradise because, he said, he went through Purgatory to find it. He successfully operated one of Iowa's early flour mills in nearby Bellevue. A collector and lover of books, he established what is considered Iowa's first library, which has been carefully preserved as it was nearly 150 years ago.

Paradise Cornbread

Yields 16 pieces   1.8 grams of fat per piece

- 1 cup yellow cornmeal
- ½ teaspoon salt
- ½ teaspoon baking soda
- 1 cup non-fat yogurt
- 1 cup cream-style corn
- 2 tablespoons skim milk
- ¼ cup egg substitute
- 2 tablespoons vegetable oil
- Vegetable cooking spray

1. Combine the cornmeal, salt and soda in a medium bowl.
2. Add the yogurt, corn, milk, egg substitute and oil. Stir until all ingredients are moistened.
3. Pour the batter into an 8x8-inch baking pan that has been coated with cooking spray.
4. Bake at 350° for 35-40 minutes or until a knife inserted in the middle comes out clean.

Bread and Breakfast

Ron Roberts, a University of Northern Iowa professor, has written the book *Iowa's Ethnic Roots* to help dispel the "homogeneous white-bread view of Iowa that just ain't so." With the help of UNI undergraduates, he studied the backgrounds of the state's many nationalities and cultures to prove that Iowa is really a state built on ethnic diversity.

Best White Bread Recipe for a Bread Machine

Bread machines take the guesswork out of how much to knead the dough or how long to let it rise. A friend who uses her machine frequently says this basic recipe gives her the most consistently good bread. She often substitutes 1/2 cup of whole-wheat flour for an equal amount of unbleached flour called for in the recipe.

Yields 1 loaf   *Less than 1 gram of fat per slice*

- ¾ cup ice water
- 1 tablespoon melted margarine
- 2 cups Pillsbury's Better for Bread or unbleached flour
- 1 teaspoon salt
- 2 tablespoons sugar
- 1 tablespoon non-fat dry milk
- 1-1½ teaspoons dry yeast.

1. Place the ice water and cooled melted margarine in the bread pan of the machine.
2. Add the flour, salt, sugar and dry milk. Add the yeast on top of dry ingredients. Do not mix.
3. Close the lid of the bread machine. Plug in the machine and push the Start button.

Bread and Breakfast

Dilly Bread

This is an especially tasty bread that is easy to make. It is low in fat and is good to have on hand when threatened with a hunger attack that might lead to snacking on high-fat chips or cookies.

Yields 2 loaves   ½ gram of fat per slice

1 cake yeast
¼ cup warm water (90°)
1 cup low-fat cottage cheese
2 tablespoons sugar
1 tablespoon onion flakes
1 tablespoon melted margarine

2 teaspoons dill seed
¼ teaspoon soda
1 teaspoon salt
¼ cup egg substitue
2¼ cups flour

1. Combine the yeast and warm water. Allow to stand for about 10 minutes.
2. Combine the remaining ingredients, except flour, and add to the yeast mixture. Mix in the flour gradually. Turn out on a floured board. Knead until the dough is smooth. Put in a large bowl and cover with a damp cloth.
3. Let rise in a warm place (about 85°) for 50-60 minutes or until double in size.
4. Turn out onto the floured board, knead and divide into equal parts. Place in two small greased bread pans. Cover and let rise until double in size.
5. Bake for 35-40 minutes at 350°. Allow to stand for 5-10 minutes after removing from the oven. Turn out onto a rack to cool.

Bread and Breakfast

Green's Sugar Bush, owned by Dale and Helen Green of Castalia, is one of Iowa's oldest family-run industries. The Green family moved to Iowa in the early 1850's and settled near Castalia in northeast Iowa. This small area was missed by the glacier that covered the rest of Iowa during the Ice Age, making it the only place in the state where the hard maple trees that produce maple sugar sap are found. The Greens who live on Green's Farm today are the fifth generation to tap the maple trees early every spring. Teams of horses pull large tanks through the timber to gather the sap for syrup making. It takes 40 gallons of sap to make 1 gallon of the delicious golden brown syrup.

Three-Grain Griddle Cakes

We met the Lovealls of Waterloo while traveling, and the conversation turned to good Iowa cooking. They told us about the wonderful maple syrup from Castalia, and I asked Sue what she liked to serve with the syrup. These thin, tender pancakes made from her recipe have become a breakfast favorite. With the mix on hand, it takes only minutes to whip up a batch. If you have Green's Sugar Bush Pure Maple Syrup to pour over the stack, they'll taste even better

Yields 60 pancakes   0 grams of fat

GRIDDLE CAKE MIX:
- 1 cup rye flour
- 1 cup whole-wheat flour
- 2 cups all-purpose flour
- ½ cup corn meal
- ⅓ cup sugar
- 2 tablespoons baking powder
- 2 teaspoons salt
- ½ teaspoon baking soda

1. Mix the dry ingredients together. Refrigerate in an airtight jar or canister.
2. When ready to make the pancakes, use the following recipe.

Bread and Breakfast

Yields 6 pancakes   2.2 grams of fat per pancake

GRIDDLE CAKES:
½ cup low-fat milk
¼ cup egg substitute or 1 egg
1 tablespoon vegetable oil
½ cup Griddle Cake Mix

1. Combine milk, egg substitute and oil.
2. Add the dry ingredient mix to milk mixture and blend well.
3. Cook on a medium-hot griddle coated with cooking spray until cakes are browned on both sides.

Bread and Breakfast

Whole-Wheat Crêpes with Nectarines

Tender whole-wheat crêpes make a delicious wrap for any number of fruit fillings, and the nectarine sauce given here is the perfect accompaniment. The recipe comes from a special friend, Mary Siberell, whose artistic flair is evident in everything she does. Many of our special memories center around meals shared with the Siberells, both at their home in Des Moines and their lake cottage at Clear Lake.

Yields 8 crepês   .7 grams of fat per crepe

WHOLE-WHEAT CRÊPES:
- ¼ cup egg substitute
- 2 tablespoons reduced-calorie margarine, melted
- 1 cup skim milk
- ½ cup whole-wheat flour
- 1 tablespoon NutraSweet Spoonful
- ¼ teaspoon vanilla
- ⅛ teaspoon salt
- Vegetable cooking spray

1. Beat the egg substitute, margarine and milk together in a medium bowl.
2. Add the flour, NutraSweet Spoonful, vanilla and salt; mix until smooth. The batter may be prepared to this point and refrigerated until ready to use.
3. Coat a 7-inch crepe pan or nonstick skillet with the cooking spray. Heat the pan over medium heat for 1-2 minutes or until hot but not smoking.
4. Pour in about 2 tablespoons batter, then quickly tilt and turn pan so the bottom is coated with a thin, even layer of batter.
5. Cook until the edges of the crêpe begin to brown and it can be easily loosened from the bottom of pan
6. Flip the crêpe and cook for another 20 seconds or until done.
7. Respray the pan before making the next crêpe.

Breads and Breakfast

NECTARINE SAUCE:

2 cups ripe nectarines, diced
½ cup apple juice (reserve ¼ cup)
1 tablespoon lemon juice
2 teaspoons cornstarch
¼ teaspoon almond extract
3 tablespoons NutraSweet Spoonful

1. Combine the nectarines, ¼ cup of apple juice and lemon juice in a medium saucepan. Cook until fruit begins to soften.
2. Combine the remaining apple juice with the cornstarch and stir into the nectarine mixture.
3. Cook for about 3 minutes or until thickened.
4. Remove from heat. Stir in the almond extract and the NutraSweet Spoonful.
5. To serve, spoon the nectarine mixture evenly over half of each crêpe and fold crêpe over. Top with another spoonful of nectarine mixture.

Note: Both the Nectarine Sauce and the Whole-Wheat Crêpes can be made ahead and reheated when entertaining. After cooking crêpes, place them on paper towels to cool; then stack between layers of waxpaper. Reheat in a microwave for 20-30 seconds or until warm.

Bread and Breakfast

Banana-Nut Bread

We took a favorite recipe and replaced half the margarine with buttermilk or yogurt and used egg substitute instead of 2 eggs. This removed half the fat and changed the taste and texture of the bread very little.

Makes 1 large loaf   *2.5 grams of fat per slice*

½ cup white sugar
½ cup brown sugar
¼ cup margarine
½ cup egg substitute
¼ cup non-fat yogurt or butter milk
3 ripe bananas, mashed

1 teaspoon soda
¼ teaspoon baking powder
2 cups flour less 2 tablespoons
¼ teaspoon salt
½ cup chopped walnuts or pecans (optional)

1. Mix the sugars, margarine and egg substitute until creamy.
2. Add the buttermilk or yogurt and the bananas. Mix well.
3. Sift the dry ingredients together and add to the banana mixture.
4. Add the nuts and stir gently until mixed.
5. Pour into a greased 9x5-inch loaf pan and bake at 350° for 1 hour or until an inserted wooden pick comes out clean.
6. Cool. Slice into ¼-inch slices.

Soups and Salads

Soups and Salads

Corn was already here when Columbus reached America. It was introduced to the new arrivals by the Indians, who grew and used it as a staple part of their diet. Early settlers in Iowa discovered that the rich soil of their region was ideal for the crop. Most of the corn in Iowa is field corn produced for livestock feed; only a small percentage is sweet corn for people to eat.

Iowa Corn Chowder

Serves 8 .2 grams of fat per serving

1 cup onion, chopped
1 cup celery, chopped
½ cup diced green pepper
3 cloves garlic, minced
2 teaspoons canola oil
¼ cup flour
2½ cups chicken broth
1½ cups water
2 carrots, chopped

2 cups peeled, diced potatoes
½ teaspoon white pepper
Salt to taste
½ teaspoon oregano
1 12-ounce can evaporated skim milk
1 17-ounce can cream-style corn
1 12-ounce can whole-kernel corn
Fresh parsley, chopped

1. In a large saucepan, sauté the onion, celery, green pepper and garlic in the oil until soft.
2. Stir in the flour and cook over medium heat until it begins to brown. Slowly add the chicken broth, stirring constantly.
3. Add the water, carrots, potatoes, white pepper, salt and oregano. Cook over low heat until potatoes are tender.
4. Stir in the evaporated milk and corn and bring to a boil.
5. Ladle into soup bowls and garnish with chopped parsley.

Soups and Salads

Potato Soup with Green Chilies

This wonderful soup is a de-fatted version of our favorite potato soup. Potatoes have only a trace of fat so can be used freely in low-fat cooking

Serves 16-18   Less than 1 gram of fat per serving

- 1 medium onion, chopped
- 2 tablespoons margarine
- 5 pounds russet potatoes, peeled and cubed
- 8 cups chicken broth
- 1 teaspoon cumin
- 1/4 - 1/2 cup chopped green chilies
- Pinch of baking soda to prevent curdling
- 3 cups evaporated skimmed milk
- Salt and pepper to taste
- Low-fat sour cream
- Chopped green onions or parsley

1. In a large soup kettle, sauté the onion in the margarine until tender.
2. Add the potatoes, chicken broth and cumin. Cover and cook for 20-30 minutes until the potatoes are tender.
3. If you like your potato soup chunky, mash the potatoes with a potato masher. If you prefer your soup smooth, blend in a food processor or blender. Return mixture to the kettle.
4. Add the green chiles, soda and evaporated milk.
5. Stir well, add the salt and pepper as desired, and simmer for another 15 minutes, stirring frequently.
6. Garnish with the low-fat sour cream and chopped green onions or parsley.

Soups and Salads

Hearty Vegetable Soup

This vegetable-packed soup is one of our favorite meatless meals. It is wonderful served with oven-toasted French bread and a tossed green salad. Make the soup the day before you plan to serve it and refrigerate it overnight. Any fat will come to the top and solidify, making it easy to remove.

Serves 8   2 grams of fat per serving

- 2 tablespoons margarine
- 1 large onion, minced
- 2 cloves garlic, minced
- 4 medium carrots, diced
- 2 large celery ribs with leaves, diced
- ½ medium head cabbage, shredded
- 2 medium potatoes, diced
- 6 cups beef or chicken stock
- 1 14½-ounce can stewed tomatoes
- 1 12-ounce can sweet corn
- ⅛ teaspoon dried oregano
- ¼ teaspoon dried basil
- Salt and pepper to taste

1. Melt the margarine in a heavy 6-quart sauce pan over medium heat.
2. Add the onions, garlic, carrots and celery. Stir and cook for about 5 minutes.
3. Add remaining ingredients, cover and simmer over low heat for 1 hour.
4. Taste to correct seasonings.

Soups and Salads

Pesto Tomato Broth

Caroline Levine of Des Moines has the knack of entertaining beautifully with little apparent effort. She serves this broth, either hot or cold, as an appetizer or as part of a meal. The pesto is special and can be used to enhance the flavor of soups, pastas and dips or as a dunk for good bread. If pine nuts aren't available, toasted sunflower seed kernels may be used.

Serves 3 ½ gram of fat per serving

- 1 10½-ounce can consommé or beef broth
- 1 11½-ounce can V8 vegetable juice
- 1 teaspoon sugar
- 2 teaspoons pesto

1. Combine ingredients in a medium saucepan.
2. Bring to a simmer. Ladle into bowls or serving mugs.

CAROLINE'S PESTO:
- 1 cup packed fresh basil leaves
- 1 large clove fresh garlic, peeled
- ½ cup olive oil
- ¼ cup pine nuts, toasted
- ½ cup freshly grated Parmesan cheese

1. Place the basil leaves and garlic in the bowl of your food processor. Add the oil gradually, scraping down the sides of the bowl as needed.
2. Add the pine nuts and Parmesan cheese and process until the mixture is blended.

Soups and Salads

Garden Gazpacho

Serve icy cold in chilled glass mugs on a hot summer day.

Serves 6   4.5 grams of fat per serving

- 2 cups tomato juice
- 1 cup fresh chopped tomatoes, peeled
- ½ cup chopped green pepper
- ½ cup chopped celery
- ½ cup chopped cucumber
- ¼ cup chopped onion
- 1 tablespoon fresh minced parsley
- 1 clove garlic, minced
- 2 tablespoons white wine vinegar
- 2 tablespoons salad oil
- 1 teaspoon salt
- ½ teaspoon Worcestershire sauce
- 4 drops Tabasco sauce
- ¼ teaspoon pepper

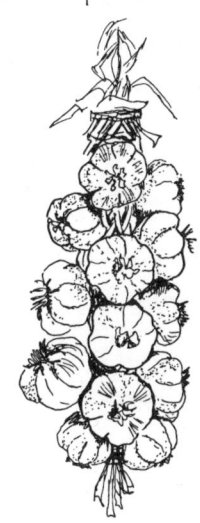

1. Place all the ingredients in a food processor or blender container.
2. Blend for 30 seconds or until thoroughly mixed but not completely smooth. Chill and serve.

♥ Garlic not only adds wonderful flavor to foods but it is good for you. Studies showed that people who ate the equivalent of 10 cloves of garlic each day had a 14% decline in cholesterol. Even better, it raised the HDL, or "good" cholesterol, and reduced the LDL, or "bad" cholesterol.

Soups and Salads

Herbert Hoover, 31st President of the United States and native of West Branch, was the first United States president to be born west of the Mississippi River. The two-room cottage where he was born and the Presidential Library are part of the Herbert Hoover National Historic Site in West Branch. Will Rogers once said, "I always did want to see Herbert Hoover elected. I wanted to see how far a competent man could go in politics. It has never been tried before." Of course, this competent man went on to become the scapegoat for many of the problems of the Great Depression.

Fresh Dilled Cucumbers

Serves 6   0 grams of fat per serving

2 tablespoons sugar
¼ cup water
½ cup vinegar

2 large cucumbers
Freshly ground black pepper
Fresh chopped dill

1. Combine the sugar and water in a small saucepan. Stir over medium heat until sugar is dissolved. Add the vinegar and let cool.
2. Peel the cucumbers and cut into ¼ inch-thick slices. Place in a medium bowl.
5. Pour the vinegar mixture over the cucumber slices. Add the black pepper and dill.
6. Refrigerate for 3-4 hours.

Soups and Salads

Garden Tomatoes With Cucumber

Serves 4   3.5 grams of fat per serving

- 4 medium tomatoes, cut into wedges
- 1 cup thinly sliced cucumber
- ½ green pepper, cut into julienne strips
- 4 thinly sliced green onions
- 3 tablespoons white wine vinegar
- 1 tablespoon olive oil
- 1 tablespoon water
- ½ teaspoon sugar
- 2 cloves garlic, minced
- ½ tablespoon fresh basil
- 1 teaspoon fresh oregano
- Salt and pepper

1. Combine the tomatoes, cucumber, green pepper and green onion in a medium bowl.
2. Combine vinegar, oil, water, sugar, garlic, basil and oregano in a jar with a lid and shake.
3. Pour over the vegetables and toss gently.
4. Refrigerate for 1-2 hours.
5. When ready to serve, add the salt and pepper. Transfer to a serving bowl lined with leaf lettuce.

Soups and Salads

Strawberry-Spinach Salad

Phyllis Conrad of Cedar Rapids contributes the recipe for this salad, which has an intriguing combination of flavors. You'll want to try it when the strawberries are at their best.

Serves 6   9.5 grams of fat per serving

- 6 cups fresh spinach (about 8 ounces)
- 1 teaspoon toasted sesame seeds
- 2 cups fresh strawberries
- ¼ cup salad oil
- 2 tablespoons red wine vinegar
- 1½ tablespoons sugar
- 1½ teaspoons minced fresh dill or ½ teaspoon dried dillweed
- ⅛ teaspoon onion powder
- ⅛ teaspoon garlic powder
- ⅛ teaspoon dry mustard
- ⅛ teaspoon salt (optional)

1. Wash the spinach carefully and remove any stems and heavy veins. Tear into bite-sized pieces. Place in a large bowl.
2. Sprinkle with the toasted sesame seeds.
3. Cut any large strawberries into halves or quarters. Add the strawberries to the spinach.
4. Combine the remaining ingredients in a screw-top jar. Cover and shake to mix. Chill. Shake again before using.
5. Pour the dressing over the spinach mixture and toss gently.

Soups and Salads

Bobbie's Spinach Salad

The ingredients in this wonderful salad combine to give it an oriental flavor

Serves 4   7 grams of fat per serving

- 10 ounces fresh spinach
- 1 5-ounce can sliced water chestnuts
- 1 10-ounce can mandarin oranges, drained
- 1 cup white grapes

DRESSING:
- 2 tablespoons low-sodium soy sauce
- 2 tablespoons rice vinegar
- 2 tablespoons frozen apple juice concentrate
- 2 tablespoons olive oil

1. Wash the spinach carefully, removing the stems and large veins. Pat dry and refrigerate for several hours before serving.
2. Tear the spinach into bite-sized pieces; combine with the water chestnuts, mandarin oranges and grapes in a large bowl.
3. Combine the dressing ingredients and mix well.
4. When ready to serve, add enough dressing to lightly coat the salad ingredients. (You will probably have some dressing left for another day).

Soups and Salads

Tangy Citrus Salad

Serves 9   4.7 grams of fat per serving

VINAIGRETTE DRESSING:

- 1 bunch red-leaf lettuce
- ½ bunch romaine lettuce
- 1 red grapefruit
- 2 large oranges
- 1 small red onion, sliced
- 1 cup jicama sticks

- 2 tablespoons cider vinegar
- 2 tablespoons orange juice
- 2 tablespoons vegetable oil
- 1 teaspoon Dijon mustard
- 1 teaspoon sugar
- ¼ teaspoon salt

1. Wash the lettuce, drain and dry by patting with paper towels. Refrigerate for several hours before serving.
2. Peel the grapefruit and oranges with a sharp knife, removing both the outer skin and the inner white pith.
3. Cut out each section so it is free of membrane.
4. When ready to assemble the salad, tear the lettuce into bite-sized pieces. Combine with the fruit, onion and jicama in a large bowl.
5. Combine the ingredients for the dressing. Pour over the greens and toss lightly.

Soups and Salads

Maize, or common corn, is the ancestor of the hybrid corn grown by today's Iowa farmer. It is a staple in the diet of over 200 million people in Third World countries. In 1970 Iowan Norman Borlaug won the Nobel Peace Prize for his part in "the green revolution," which led to increases in both the nutrient values and the yields of corn through research of new and better strains. These improved types of corn have been important in bringing better nutrition to starving millions in Africa and South and Central America.

Corn and Black Bean Salad

Iowa cooks have found that the flavor and color of black beans go beautifully with corn. They are a welcome addition to a healthy diet because they have lots of fiber and almost no fat or cholesterol.

Serves 6   8 grams of fat per serving

- 1 16-ounce can black beans
- 1 16½-ounce can whole-kernel corn
- ½ cup chopped red bell pepper
- 3 green onions, chopped (including tops)
- 2 cloves garlic, minced
- ¼ cup chopped fresh parsley
- ¼ cup chopped walnuts or pecans
- 2 tablespoons olive oil
- 2 tablespoons soy sauce
- 3 tablespoons lemon juice
- 1 tablespoon whole-grain mustard

1. Drain the beans and corn and place in a large bowl.
2. Add the chopped red pepper, green onions, garlic, parsley and nuts.
3. Combine the olive oil, soy sauce, lemon juice and mustard in a small jar with a lid. Shake well.
4. Pour the dressing over the bean mixture and stir gently. Cover and marinate in the refrigerator for several hours before serving.

Soups and Salads

Calico Salad

This colorful, crisp salad with a sweet-sour dressing has no fat. It is easy to prepare and comes from Helen Westcot of Cedar Rapids.

Serves 8   0 grams of fat per serving

DRESSING:
- ½ - ¾ cup sugar (less if you like your salad tart)
- ½ cup vinegar
- 1 tablespoon prepared mustard
- 1 heaping tablespoon flour
- Pinch of salt

VEGETABLES:
- 4 stalks of celery, chopped fine
- ½ green pepper, chopped fine
- 1 medium onion, chopped fine
- 1 10-ounce package frozen mixed vegetables, cooked as directed and drained
- 1 16-ounce can dark red kidney beans, drained

1. Combine the dressing ingredients in a medium saucepan.
2. Bring to a boil over medium heat; cook and stir until the mixture is bubbly and clear.
3. Combine the vegetables in a medium bowl.
4. Pour the dressing over the vegetables; toss to mix.
5. Cover and refrigerate. Allow 2-3 hours for flavors to blend.

Soups and Salad

Okoboji Five-Bean Salad

Serves 16 2 grams of fat per serving

- 1 16-ounce can green beans
- 1 16-ounce can wax beans
- 1 15-ounce can kidney beans
- 1 16-ounce can garbanzo beans
- 1 16-ounce can pinto beans
- ½ cup chopped green pepper
- ½ cup chopped celery
- ½ cup finely chopped onion
- ⅓ cup sugar
- ⅔ cup terragon vinegar
- 2 tablespoons canola oil
- ½ teaspoon salt
- ½ teaspoon garlic salt

1. Combine the vegetables in a large bowl.
2. Mix the sugar, vinegar, oil, salt and garlic salt.
3. Pour the dressing mixture over the vegetables and stir gently.
4. Refrigerate for several hours, stirring several times to blend flavors evenly.

Rice & Bean Salad

Serves 12 1 gram of fat per serving

- 1 16-ounce can pinto beans
- 1 16-ounce can black beans
- 3 cups cooked rice
- 1 10-ounce package frozen green peas, thawed but not cooked
- 1 cup sliced celery
- 1 cup chopped onion
- 2 4-ounce cans chopped green chilies
- 1 8-ounce bottle low-fat Italian salad dressing

1. Drain the beans. Combine the beans, rice, peas, celery, onion and green chilies in a large bowl.
2. Pour the Italian salad dressing over the ingredients in the bowl and toss.
3. Cover and refrigerate for 24 hours before serving.

Soups and Salads

Jo's New Potato Salad

When Jo Sloan moved from Fort Madison to Des Moines several years ago, Des Moines gained a superb cook and hostess. After her husband, Chet, developed heart problems, she used her talent and cooking expertise to change their diet to one low in fat. Her food still tastes wonderful; this potato salad is just an example.

Serves 10-12   5.5 grams of fat per serving

- 4 pounds (about 16) new potatoes
- ½ cup chopped red bell pepper
- ½ cup chopped green bell pepper
- ¼ cup chopped celery
- ¼ cup chopped red onion
- ¼ cup chopped chives
- 2 tablespoons minced parsley
- ¼ cup Puritan oil
- 2 tablespoons red wine vinegar
- 1 tablespoon chopped fresh thyme or 1 teaspoon dried thyme
- Salt and pepper to taste

1. Scrub the potatoes and cook in salted water for 20-25 minutes or until potatoes are tender but still firm.
2. Drain and cool. Cut into bite-sized pieces and place in a large bowl.
3. Add the chopped peppers, celery, onions and herbs.
4. Combine the oil, vinegar, thyme, salt and pepper. Add to the potato mixture.
5. Toss gently until all the vegetables are thoroughly coated.
6. Serve at room temperature.

Soups and Salads

San's Dilled Potato Salad

A mutual friend told me about this wonderful cook named San Anderson from Clinton. When I contacted San, she said, "I'm in big trouble because I don't cook low-fat." She then proceeded to share several recipes - all low-fat. The dill and mustard in her recipe add a special tang; and the tender peel left on the new potatoes adds texture, nutrients and eye appeal.

Serves 8   6 grams of fat per serving

- 1½ pounds (7 or 8) small new red potatoes, unpeeled
- ⅓ cup sliced green onions
- 1 cup Hellmann's Reduced Fat mayonnaise
- 1 tablespoon prepared yellow mustard
- 1½ teaspoons dill weed
- ½ teaspoon salt
- ½ teaspoon black pepper

1. Cook the potatoes, cool and cut into bite-sized chunks.
2. Place the potatoes in a medium bowl. Add the green onions.
3. Combine the mayonnaise, mustard, dill weed, salt and pepper and gently stir into potato mixture.
4. Refrigerate for several hours so flavors have a chance to blend.

> ♥ *You can reduce the fat content to 4.5 grams per serving by substituting ½ cup low-fat sour cream and 1 tablespoon vinegar for ½ cup of the mayonnaise.*

Main Events

Main Event

Pecan Chicken Breasts

The pecan and bread crumbs combination gives such a wonderful flavor and crunch to this chicken that you'll stop yearning for the golden fried chicken you once enjoyed for Sunday dinner in Iowa. When Sunday came, Iowa cooks weren't content unless every inch of the table was covered with bowls and platters heaped with chicken, fragrant rolls, fluffy mashed potatoes, gravy, fruit salads, home-grown vegetables, pies, cakes and homemade jellies, relishes and pickles. That was before we gave much thought to calories, fat content or cholesterol.

Serves 4   15 grams of fat per serving

- 4 chicken breasts, skinned and boned
- 1 cup bread crumbs
- ¼ cup finely chopped pecans
- ¾ cup flour
- Salt to taste
- ¼ teaspoon black pepper
- ½ cup egg substitute
- 1 tablespoon water
- 2 dashes Tabasco sauce
- Vegetable cooking spray
- 2 tablespoons margarine

1. Trim any fat from the chicken breasts.
2. Mix the bread crumbs and pecans in a flat bowl. Sprinkle the flour on a dinner plate and season with salt and pepper.
3. Beat the egg substitute, water and Tabasco sauce in a medium bowl.
4. Dip the chicken breasts first in the flour, then in the egg mixture, then in the bread crumb mixture. Place on a plate and chill for at least 30 minutes.
5. When ready to cook, coat a large nonstick skillet with cooking spray. Melt the margarine over medium heat. Add the chicken breasts and cook for about 30 minutes, turning to brown evenly on all sides. Lower heat if chicken begins to brown too fast. Respray with cooking spray if necessary.

Main Event

The Maytag name first became known for the washing machines manufactured in the mid-Iowa town of Newton. To Iowans and cheese lovers, however, the name Maytag brings to mind the wonderful blue cheese made at the Maytag Dairy Farms. The dairy farm became more than a hobby of the Maytag family when Iowa State University, working with Frederick Maytag, developed and patented their blue cheese process in the early 1940's.

Chicken Maytag Blue

The rich flavor of Maytag Blue Cheese combined with spinach in the filling of the chicken rolls makes a memorable taste treat. The recipe was contributed by Jim Stevens, President of the Maytag Dairy Farms

Serves 6   8 grams of fat per serving

- 1½ cups rice
- 6 skinned, boned chicken breast halves
- 1 10-ounce package frozen chopped spinach
- 1 tablespoon olive oil
- 1 clove garlic, finely minced or crushed
- 2 ounces Maytag Blue Cheese
- Ground pepper to taste
- 2 tablespoons fresh, chopped parsley or 1 teaspoon dried parsley
- Soy sauce
- 2 tablespoons fine dry bread crumbs

1. Cook the rice according to directions on the package. Set aside.
2. Place the chicken between 2 sheets of waxed paper or heavy-duty plastic wrap. Flatten with a meat mallet or a rolling pin until about ¼-inch thick.
3. Drain the spinach and squeeze until nearly dry.
4. Heat the oil in a nonstick skillet. Add the garlic, spinach, pepper and Maytag Blue Cheese. Cook over medium heat, stirring constantly, until the cheese is melted (2-3 minutes).

Main Event

5. Divide the spinach mixture among the chicken cutlets, folding the chicken around the filling and tucking the ends under.
6. Season the cooked rice with the parsley and place in an oiled, oven-proof dish.
7. Place the chicken rolls seam-side down on the rice. Brush the top of the chicken rolls lightly with soy sauce. Sprinkle with bread crumbs.
8. Cover the dish and bake at 375° for 35 minutes or until the chicken is tender.

Pan-Grilled Chicken Breasts

Rolling or pounding the chicken breasts so they are uniformly thick reduces the cooking time. This quick-and-easy way to prepare chicken has become one of our favorites. The fat per serving can be reduced even more by substituting low-fat Italian salad dressing for some of the oil.

Serves 4   8 grams of fat per serving

- 4 (4-ounce) skinned, boned chicken breast halves
- 2 tablespoons vegetable oil
- 2 tablespoons reduced-sodium soy sauce
- 1 teaspoon grated fresh ginger
- 2 cloves garlic, minced

1. Place the chicken breasts between two pieces of heavy-duty plastic wrap, and flatten with a meat mallet or rolling pin to 1/4-inch thickness.
2. Combine the oil, soy sauce, ginger and garlic and brush over both sides of chicken breasts. Marinate for at least 30 minutes.
3. Coat a large nonstick skillet with cooking spray and place over medium heat until hot.
4. Add chicken and cook on each side for 4 minutes or until browned.

Main Event

Chicken & Stuffing Casserole

If your family loves the stuffing best when you roast a chicken or turkey, you will want to try this recipe. Turkey is good when used instead of the chicken and gives you 4 grams of fat per serving. It's almost like having Thanksgiving dinner and a lot less trouble.

Serves 8   6 grams of fat per serving

- Vegetable cooking spray
- 1 tablespoon margarine
- ½ cup chopped celery
- ½ cup chopped onion
- 2 cups chicken broth
- 1 10¾-ounce can Campbell's Healthy Request Cream of Chicken Soup
- 1 10¾-ounce can Campbell's Healthy Request Cream of Mushroom soup
- 1 8-ounce package Pepperidge Farm Herb Seasoned Stuffing Mix
- 4 large skinless chicken breasts, cooked and cubed

1. Coat a large skillet with cooking spray. Add the margarine, celery and onion and sauté over medium heat until tender.
2. Combine the broth and soups in a large bowl. Reserve 1 cup of the soup mixture for the topping.
3. Combine the stuffing mix, celery and onion with the soups.
4. Layer half of the stuffing mixture in the bottom of a 9x13-inch casserole that has been coated with cooking spray.
5. Spread half of the cooked chicken over top of stuffing mixture. Repeat process with remaining stuffing and chicken.
6. Top with reserved soup mixture. Cover with foil and bake at 350° for 45 minutes.

Main Event

New Chicken Fricassee

Chicken fricassee was a favorite Sunday dinner at our house when I was a child. Some recipes can be converted to low-fat without sacrificing taste, and this tastes as good as I remember my mother making it, but it has a lot less calories and fat.

Serves 6   11 grams of fat per serving

- Vegetable cooking spray
- 6 4-ounce chicken breast halves, skinned
- 2 tablespoons margarine
- 2 cups chicken broth
- 1 cup sliced celery
- 1 cup chopped onion
- 2 cups baby carrots
- 2 cups sliced fresh mushrooms
- 2 envelopes Lipton Cream of Chicken Cup-a-Soup Mix
- 1 7.5-ounce tube ready-to-bake low-fat biscuits

1. Coat a large nonstick skillet with cooking spray and place over medium heat. Melt the margarine. Add the chicken and cook until lightly browned.
2. Remove the chicken from the skillet and place it in a 3-quart casserole.
3. Pour ½ cup of the chicken broth into the skillet; simmer and stir to loosen any crusty bits of chicken in the pan. Combine the Lipton's Cup-a-Soup Mix and the remaining chicken broth in the skillet. Stir and simmer for 2-3 minutes or until broth thickens.
4. Combine the celery, onion, carrots and mushrooms with the mixture in the skillet. Simmer briefly.
5. Spoon the vegetables and broth mixture over the chicken breast. Cover. Bake at 300° for 30 minutes.
6. Remove the casserole from the oven, uncover and place the unbaked biscuits on top of the hot fricassee.
7. Increase the oven temperature to 375°. Return the casserole to the oven and bake, uncovered, for another 20 minutes or until the biscuits are nicely browned.

Main Event

Flat-Out Garlic Chicken

My sister, Rena, brought this recipe for microwaved chicken on her last visit. She said "It's different but really good and you need it for your cookbook." Trust the instructions for laying the chicken "flat out" and you'll have an attractive main dish. The 20 cloves of garlic in the sauce may sound like a lot, but the flavor is quite subtle.

Serves 4   10 grams of fat per serving.

3 to 4 pound fryer
20 large garlic cloves, unpeeled
2 tablespoons melted margarine
½ cup dry vermouth
Salt and pepper to taste

1.. Remove the skin from the chicken. Use heavy kitchen shears to cut through both sides of the backbone and neck portion. Remove and save for soup.
2. Spread the chicken, cavity side down, on a large cutting board.
3. "Whack" the center of breast with the palm of your hand to flatten the chicken. Tuck the wings under the shoulders and turn legs so outside part is facing up.
4. Place the unpeeled garlic cloves in the bottom of a large microwaveable baking dish.
5. Arrange the chicken, cavity side down, on top of the garlic cloves and brush with melted margarine. Add seasonings and vermouth.
6. Cover the dish with plastic film wrap or wax paper, puncturing several small holes in cover for steam to escape. Microwave on High for 22-25 minutes.
7. Remove the chicken to a serving dish and drain the pan juices into a blender or processor. Squeeze the garlic meat into the juices and puree. (The garlic meat will pop out easily and husks can be discarded.)
8. Pour the sauce over the chicken, garnish and serve.

Main Event

Turkey Cutlets With Lemon Sauce

This conversion of a recipe for Veal Piccata offers a different approach to cooking turkey. The sauce with lemon juice and capers is easy to prepare and adds a real zing to the turkey cutlets.

Serves 4   10.5 grams of fat per serving

4 4-ounce turkey cutlets
¼ cup all-purpose flour
½ teaspoon salt
½ teaspoon black pepper
Vegetable cooking spray
1 tablespoon olive oil

1 clove garlic, minced
½ cup chicken broth
1 tablespoon lemon juice
1 tablespoon capers, drained
Fresh parsley, chopped

1. Flatten the turkey cutlets by covering with waxed paper and tapping lightly with one side of a rolling pin until cutlets are about ¼-inch thick.
2. Mix the flour, salt and pepper on a plate. Dredge the cutlets lightly in the mixture.
3. Coat a nonstick skillet with the cooking spray. Add the oil and heat. Cook the cutlets in the oil until browned, about 2-3 minutes on each side.
4. Remove the cutlets to a warmed plate to hold.
5. Add the garlic to the pan and sauté briefly. Add the chicken broth; simmer and stir to loosen any browned bits of cutlet in the pan. The flour used in dredging the cutlets will thicken the sauce slightly.
6. Stir in the lemon juice and capers and simmer for 1-2 minutes.
7. Spoon the sauce over the cutlets, sprinkle with the parsley and serve.

Main Event

Glazed Turkey Breast

This is the easiest way I know to have beautiful slices of moist turkey breast for a delicious low-fat main course.

Serves 8-10   4 grams of fat per serving

1 6 to 7- pound turkey breast
⅓ cup honey
1 tablespoon dry mustard

1 6½- ounce can frozen apple juice (undiluted)

1. Preheat the oven to 325°.
2. Remove the skin from the turkey breast and insert a meat thermometer into the center of the breast.
3. Combine the honey, dry mustard and apple juice.
4. Place the turkey breast in a large roasting pan. Baste the entire breast generously with the apple juice mixture.
5. Cover the turkey breast and bake for 1 hour.
6. Uncover and bake for another hour or until meat thermometer registers 180°. Baste frequently after removing cover from turkey.
7. Remove from the oven and allow to cool for 15-20 minutes before slicing.

A suggested rule of entertaining is to serve a lowered-fat menu if you have eight or more guests. At least one will be on a low-fat diet, and one or two more should be. There is no better way to show your friends you care about them.

Main Event

The Iowa State Fair is one of the best fairs anywhere. The farmers, the FFA and 4-H boys and girls, and Iowa women come with their best to compete in what they do best---producing food for the world. For everyone, it's a reminder that Iowa's roots are deeply embedded in the soil of Iowa's farms.

State Fair Grilled Turkey Tenderloins

The breast meat of the turkey is very lean and should be included often in a low-fat diet. The tenderloin is the choicest part of a boned turkey breast and is delicious marinated and grilled. If turkey tenderloins are not available, you may use thick slices of boned turkey breast.

Serves 4   6 grams of fat per serving

- 4 5-ounce turkey tenderloins, ¾-inch thick
- ¼ cup reduced-sodium soy sauce
- 2 tablespoons canola oil
- ¼ cup sherry wine
- 2 tablespoons lemon juice
- 2 tablespoons minced onion
- ¼ teaspoon ginger
- Dash of black pepper
- Garlic salt to taste

1. Place the tenderloins between 2 pieces of wax paper. Tap lightly with a meat mallet or the side of a rolling pin until they are of uniform thickness and will cook more evenly.
2. Combine the remaining ingredients in a shallow dish. Add the turkey, turning to coat both sides.
3. Cover and refrigerate for 2-4 hours, turning occasionally.
4. Grill over medium-hot coals for 8-10 minutes on each side. The tenderloins are done if the juice runs clear when pierced with a fork. Do not overcook or the turkey will become dry and tough.

Main Event

Cornish Hens With Fruit

The rich, brown glaze formed by the marinade and brown sugar on these Cornish Game Hens makes this an elegant dish to set before your guests.

Serves 4   9 grams of fat per serving

- 2 Cornish Game Hens
- 1 cup white wine vinegar
- ⅓ cup olive oil
- 4 cloves garlic, minced
- 2 tablespoons capers with juice
- ¾ cup dried apricots
- ¾ cup dried prunes
- ½ teaspoon black pepper
- ½ teaspoon salt
- ¼ cup brown sugar

1. With a sharp knife or poultry shears, cut along the side of the breastbone and down the center of the backbone to cut the hens in half. Remove the skin.
2. Place the hens in a plastic bag.
3. Combine the vinegar, oil and garlic. Pour the marinade over the hens.
4. Add the capers, apricots and prunes. Refrigerate for 2 hours, turning occasionally.
5. Arrange the hens in a shallow roasting pan, cavity side up. Bake at 350° for 25 minutes.
6. Turn the hens over, spoon the fruit and capers around them. Add the salt and pepper to the marinade left in the bag. Baste the hens with the marinade.
7. Sprinkle the brown sugar evenly over the hens and roast for another 45 minutes. Baste carefully every 10 minutes so glaze is not disturbed.
8. Serve the hens, surrounded by the fruit and parsley, on a large platter

Main Event

Grilled Pork Tenderloins

Grilled pork tenderloins are easy to prepare when butterflied and marinated. Cook quickly so they will be tender and juicy. The marinade gives them a wonderfully tangy flavor.

Serves 6   7 grams of fat per serving

- 2 (¾-pound) pork tenderloins
- ⅓ cup low-sodium soy sauce
- 1 tablespoon olive oil
- 2 teaspoons minced garlic
- ¼ cup frozen apple juice concentrate
- 2 tablespoons brown sugar
- ½ teaspoon ground ginger
- Vegetable cooking spray

1. Butterfly the tenderloins by cutting them lengthwise to within ½ inch of the other side. Spread the two sides and place them in a shallow dish.
2. Combine the remaining ingredients, except cooking spray, and pour over the meat.
3. Marinate at room temperature for 30-45 minutes, turning every 10 minutes.
4. Heat the grill; coat the rack with cooking spray. Place the tenderloins on the rack over medium-hot coals.
5. Grill each side for 5-6 minutes depending on the thickness of the meat. If you have an instant meat thermometer, insert it into thickest part of tenderloin. The pork is done when the thermometer registers 150°. Do not overcook or the pork will become dry and tough.

Note: If you don't yet have an instant meat thermometer, make an investment in one. You can check the internal temperature of whatever you are cooking by inserting it for one minute. It is especially helpful when checking meat cooked on the grill.

Main Event

Medallions of Pork Tenderloin

Slices of pork tenderloin combined with julienne strips of green, red and yellow bell peppers make an elegant but simple-to-prepare main course.

Serves 4   8.5 grams of fat per serving

1 pound pork tenderloin
Salt and pepper to taste
Vegetable cooking spray
1 tablespoon canola oil
1 medium onion, chopped
3 sweet peppers (red, green and yellow) cut into julienne strips
1 teaspoon finely minced garlic
2 tablespoons chicken broth

1. Cut tenderloin into eight equal slices. Flatten each slice with a meat mallet until they are about ½-inch thick. Sprinkle with salt and pepper.
2. Coat a large nonstick skillet with cooking spray. Add 1 teaspoon of oil and place over medium-high heat.
3. When oil is hot, add the medallions and cook for 5 minutes on each side or until browned. They are done if the juice runs clear when pierced with a fork. Remove the medallions from the skillet and set aside.
4. Add the remaining 2 teaspoons of oil to the skillet over medium heat. Place the onion, peppers and garlic in the skillet and sauté over medium heat for 3 minutes, stirring constantly.
5. Add the chicken broth and cook and stir for another 3 minutes.
6. Spoon the peppers onto a large serving plate and arrange the medallions on top of the peppers.

Main Event

Iowa farmers are now breeding and feeding their pigs to produce meat 31% leaner than it was a few years ago. A well-trimmed 3-ounce loin chop now has only 7 grams of fat, which makes it a great addition to a low-fat diet. The Iowa Pork Producers Association's promotional material proclaims that pork is "the other white meat."

Easy-Baked Pork Chops

Serves 4   *7 grams of fat per serving*

- 4 3-ounce loin chops, all visible fat removed
- 1 green pepper, chopped
- ¼ cup chopped onion
- 2 cloves garlic, finely minced
- 1 tablespoon lemon juice
- ¼ teaspoon dried basil or 1 teaspoon chopped fresh basil
- 1½ cups stewed tomatoes

1. Arrange the pork chops in a 9x13-inch baking pan.
2. Combine the remaining ingredients and pour over the chops. Cover tightly with aluminum foil.
3. Bake at 350° for 40 minutes.

Main Event

Favorite Grilled Kabobs

When the 4 ounces of meat that is acceptable to a low-fat diet is cubed and grilled, it seems a great plenty. With the grilled vegetables it is an attractive dinner and needs nothing except a simple green salad and some good bread.

Serves 4   10 grams of fat per serving

- 1 pound top sirloin, trimmed
- ½ cup light Italian dressing
- 2 tablespoons red wine
- 1 clove garlic, minced
- 1 teaspoon Dijon mustard
- 12 cherry tomatoes
- 12 fresh mushrooms
- 4 small red unpeeled potatoes, cooked and halved
- 1 green pepper, cut into chunks
- 1 cup light Italian dressing

1. Cut the meat into 1-inch chunks, trimming as much fat as possible; place in a medium bowl.
2. Combine the Italian dressing, wine, garlic and Dijon mustard and pour over the meat. Marinate for 2-4 hours.
3. Combine the vegetables in a large bowl. Cover with the Italian dressing and marinate for 1 hour.
4. Remove the meat and vegetables from marinade and arrange on skewers.
5. Cook over hot coals for 4-5 minutes, turn and grill for another 3-4 minutes or until done to your liking.

Main Event

Iowa Standing Rib Roast

A special event may call for a pink, juicy roast not usually on your menu. This simple, dependable way to prepare a rib roast works regardless of the size of the roast. The meat will be medium-rare, juicy and rich with the flavor of Iowa cornfed beef. If you have roast left over, save the pan drippings for gravy for the next day.

Serves 10   14 grams of fat per 4-ounce serving

4 to 5 pound Iowa standing rib roast   Salt and pepper to taste

1. Wipe the roast and place it in a shallow pan, ribs down.
2. Roast, uncovered, in a preheated 350° oven for 1 hour.
3. Turn the oven off and leave the meat in the oven for at least 3 hours. **Do not open the oven door!**
4. One and one-half hours before you are ready to serve, turn oven to 350° and roast for another hour.
5. Remove from the oven; season with salt and pepper.
6. Allow the meat to rest for 20 minutes before carving. Deglaze the pan and reserve the pan drippings for later use.*

*__Defatted Beef Gravy:__ Deglaze the pan by adding ½ cup of beef broth and simmering briefly, stirring to loosen the pan drippings. Pour into a small bowl and refrigerate overnight. Remove fat that has solidified on top. You should have almost 1 cup of meat juices and broth. Place 2 tablespoons of flour in a heavy skillet and stir over medium heat until lightly browned. Remove from heat and gradually stir in the defatted meat juices. Return to heat and cook and stir until gravy is thickened, adding more beef broth as necessary. Salt and pepper to taste. Defatted gravy has only a trace of fat.

Main Event

Potter's Rosemary Swiss Steak

This quick-and-easy Swiss Steak recipe comes from Marlys Potter of Nevada, Iowa. Marlys said she once prepared a longer, more complicated version of this recipe; but she improvised once when in a hurry, and husband Jim likes her shortcut better.

Serves 4   11 grams of fat per serving

- 1 pound 1-inch-thick round steak
- 2 teaspoons vegetable oil
- Salt and pepper to taste
- ½ teaspoon dried rosemary
- 1 tablespoon Dijon mustard
- 3 large tomatoes, sliced
- 1 large onion, sliced
- ¼-½ cup water

1. Trim as much fat as possible from the meat.
2. Place the oil in a heavy skillet over medium heat. Brown the meat well on both sides.
3. Season with salt, pepper and rosemary. Spread the mustard on one side of the steak. Top with slices of tomatoes and onion.
4. Add the water, cover pan tightly and simmer slowly for 1½ hours. Check occasionally, adding more water if needed.
5. Serve with the pan juices.

> If the man in your life loves steak, let him enjoy it occasionally without guilt. Keep the size of the serving to 4 ounces and trim as much fat as you can. Stay away from prime grades of meat, because it is the marbling of fat that makes it prime. A broiled 4-ounce serving of untrimmed prime sirloin is 27 grams of fat, while the same serving of trimmed choice sirloin is 9.8 grams of fat. The top round called for in this recipe has slightly less fat than sirloin.

Main Event

Heart-Smart Meatloaf

One of our family's favorite meals is meatloaf served with baked potatoes and a green salad. It took several tries to develop a low-fat recipe that my husband really liked. The test of a good meatloaf is how it tastes later in a sandwich, and you'll want to make enough of this for sandwiches the next day.

Serves 6   6 grams of fat per serving

- 1½ pounds extra-lean ground beef (93-95% lean)
- ½ cup chopped onion
- ¼ green pepper, finely chopped
- ¾ cup Quaker Oats, quick or old-fashioned
- ¼ cup egg substitute
- 1 tablespoon prepared horseradish
- 1 teaspoon dry mustard
- ¼ cup catsup
- ¼ cup tomato juice
- 1 teaspoon Worcestershire sauce
- ½ teaspoon salt (optional)
- ¼ teaspoon pepper
- 1 cup tomato sauce

1. Combine all ingredients except the tomato sauce, which is saved for the topping. Mix with hands to thoroughly combine the ingredients.
2. Shape into a loaf and place in a 9x5-inch pan.
3. Spoon the tomato sauce over top of the loaf and bake for 1 hour at 350°. Drain fat and juices and let stand for 5 minutes before slicing and serving.

> ♥ Look for packages of ground beef marked "93%" or "95% lean." If you buy "80% lean," you will have almost 4 times the amount of fat. One pound of "95% lean" has only 24 grams of fat while one pound of "80% lean" has 91 grams of fat.

Main Event

Mrs. Martin's Meatballs with Noodles

Sour Cream Meatballs from Clara Martin in Charles City was a favorite recipe in my first cookbook. The ground beef, sour cream, butter and eggs in the recipe added up to 43 grams of fat per serving. By converting the recipe and using low-fat ingredients, there are only 9 grams of fat per serving and it is still a family favorite.

Serves 8   9 grams of fat per serving

- 2 pounds extra-lean ground beef (at least 93% fat-free)
- 1 envelope Lipton's Onion Recipe Secrets soup mix
- 1 cup bread crumbs
- ¼ cup egg substitute
- ⅓ cup flour
- Vegetable cooking spray
- 1 tablespoon vegetable oil
- 2 envelopes Lipton Cream of Chicken Cup-a-Soup
- 1½ cups water
- Egg noodles

1. Mix the extra-lean ground beef, onion soup mix, bread crumbs and egg substitute in a large bowl until well blended. Form the mixture into balls, dusting your hands lightly with flour so the meatballs are easier to handle.
2. Coat a large nonstick skillet with cooking spray, add the oil and heat. Brown the meatballs over medium heat, turning as they brown. Respray the skillet when necessary.
3. Place the meatballs on paper towels, patting with the towels to absorb any excess oil. Drain off and discard any oil left in the skillet.
4. Add 1½ cups of water to the skillet; blend in the cream of chicken soup mix, bring the mixture to a boil and simmer until thickened.
5. Transfer the meatballs back into the skillet with the soup mixture and simmer for 15 minutes, adding more water if needed.
6. Serve over cooked noodles.

Main Event

Baked Fish With Almonds

Serves 4   8 grams of fat per serving

- 2 tablespoons sliced almonds
- 1 pound fish fillets (flounder, sole or orange roughy)
- ½ cup flour
- ¼ cup Hellmann's Reduced Fat Mayonnaise
- 1 tablespoon lemon juice
- 1 cup dry bread crumbs
- 1 tablespoon melted margarine
- ½ teaspoon salt
- ¼ teaspoon dried dill weed

1. Place the almonds in a baking dish and toast in a 350° oven for 5 minutes, stirring occasionally. Set aside.
2. Dredge the fish fillets in the flour and place in a flat baking dish.
3. Combine the mayonnaise and lemon juice; spread over the top of the fish fillets.
4. Mix remaining ingredients and combine with the toasted almonds. Sprinkle over the top of the fish fillets.
5. Bake, uncovered, for 12-14 minutes at 350° or until fish flakes easily when pierced with a fork.
6. To serve, garnish with lemon slices and parsley.

Main Event

Marv's Seafood Pasta

This pasta dish is my husband's specialty and he does it beautifully. It's one of our favorite recipes when entertaining a few people for a casual evening. He does most of the chopping and mincing ahead of time, but puts it together while we visit with our guests in the kitchen.

Serves 4   7 grams of fat per serving

- 2 tablespoons olive oil
- ¾ cup chopped onion
- ¼ cup chopped green pepper
- ¼ cup chopped red pepper
- 2 large garlic cloves, minced
- 2 large ripe tomatoes, peeled and chopped
- ¼ cup chopped fresh parsley
- ½ teaspoon salt
- ½ teaspoon black pepper
- 1 pound shrimp or crab
- 16 ounces angel hair pasta
- Freshly grated Parmesan cheese

1. Heat the oil in a large saucepan. Add the onion, peppers and garlic and sauté until glossy.
2. Add the tomatoes, seasonings and seafood and cook over medium heat for 5 minutes.
3. While the seafood mixture is simmering, cook the pasta according to directions on the package.
4. Drain the pasta and transfer to a large platter. Ladle the seafood sauce over top of the pasta; sprinkle with freshly grated Parmesan cheese.

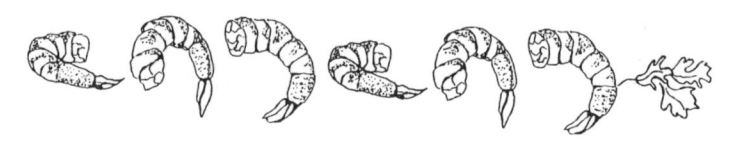

Main Event

Sautéed Scallops with Vegetables

Scallops are sweet and tender and have only a trace of fat. Freshness is important so ask your grocer which days scallops are delivered. Remember they cook quickly, and longer cooking will only make them tough.

Serves 4   2 grams of fat per serving

- 1 small carrot
- 1 small zucchini
- ½ sweet red pepper
- 1 pound fresh scallops
- Vegetable cooking spray
- 2 teaspoons oil or margarine
- 1 clove garlic, minced
- 2 cups sliced mushrooms
- ¼ cup chicken broth
- 1 teaspoon cornstarch
- Salt and pepper to taste
- 2 tablespoons chopped parsley

1. Cut the carrots, zucchini and red pepper into julienne strips. Set aside.
2. Rinse the scallops and pat dry.
3. Coat a nonstick pan with the cooking spray; add the oil. Place the pan over medium-high heat. When the oil is heated, add the scallops. Cook for 4 minutes, stirring occasionally to brown the scallops evenly.
4. Add the garlic and sauté for 1 minute. Remove from the pan and set aside.
5. Add the vegetable strips and the mushrooms to the pan with the chicken broth.
6. Place the cornstarch in a small dish. Remove 1 teaspoon broth from pan and mix with cornstarch until smooth. Return cornstarch mixture to the pan. Cook and stir over medium heat until slightly thickened.
7. Cook the vegetables for 4 to 5 minutes or until just tender.
8. Add the scallops to the vegetables and heat briefly.
9. Season to taste. Remove to a serving dish and sprinkle with chopped parsley.

Main Event

Tuna-Tomato Pita Pockets

Sun-dried tomatoes give tangy tomato flavor to this sandwich filling without the extra moisture of regular tomatoes. If you don't have sun-dried tomatoes, substitute chopped red bell peppers

Serves 4   5 grams of fat per serving

- ½ cup sun-dried tomato halves, snipped into half-inch pieces
- 2 6-ounce cans chunk light tuna in spring water, drained
- ¼ cup diced celery
- ¼ cup diced green pepper
- 4 green onions, minced
- 6 tablespoons Hellmann's Reduced Fat Mayonnaise
- 1 tablespoon prepared mustard
- 4 8-inch round pitas
- 1 cup shredded lettuce

1. Place the sun-dried tomatoes in a medium bowl. Cover with boiling water and let stand for 10-12 minutes.
2. Drain the tomatoes and pat dry with paper towels. Return them to the bowl and combine them with the tuna, celery, green pepper, onions, mayonnaise and mustard. Mix well.
3. Cut the round pitas in half and open the pockets.
4. Spoon ¼ cup of the tuna mixture into each pita pocket. Tuck in the shredded lettuce and serve immediately.

> The average cholesterol level of adult Americans dropped from 213 in 1978 to 205 in 1990 according to a recent survey published by The Journal of the American Medical Association. This means more people are closer to the 200 range considered desirable. Old habits are hard to break, but it seems that people are beginning to realize that eating right is a key to a better and longer life.

Main Event

Pasta with Broccoli-Tomato Sauce

Pasta, with 1 gram of fat per serving, is a perfect base for meatless meals. This sauce can be varied according to what's available. The Greek olives, freshly ground Parmesan cheese and fresh tomatoes add a wonderful Mediterranean flavor; however, black olives, Parmesan cheese from a shaker and canned Italian stewed tomatoes may be substituted.

4 servings   4 grams of fat per serving

2 cups fresh broccoli flowerets
2 large ripe tomatoes
Vegetable cooking spray
1 tablespoon olive oil
2 garlic cloves, minced
½ teaspoon red pepper flakes
10 Greek olives, sliced
½ cup coarsely chopped parsley
Salt and pepper to taste
½ pound angel hair pasta
Freshly grated Parmesan cheese

1. Steam the broccoli over boiling water for 3-4 minutes. Remove from heat and spray with cold water.
2. Peel the tomatoes after immersing them in boiling water for 12 seconds. The skin will slip off easily. Chop the tomatoes coarsely.
3. Coat a large nonstick skillet with the cooking spray. Add the oil and place over medium-high heat. Add the tomatoes, garlic, red pepper flakes, Greek olives, parsley, salt and pepper. Sauté for 3-4 minutes and add the broccoli. Cook for another 2 minutes.
4. Cook the pasta according to the instructions on the package. Drain and remove to a serving plate. Ladle the sauce mixture over the pasta and sprinkle with freshly grated Parmesan cheese.

Main Event

White Lasagna

When Iowans aren't in Iowa, many find that the product they miss most is Anderson Erickson Cottage Cheese. Lovers of cottage cheese try brands in other states, but none captures that special flavor. This recipe is reprinted from an AE brochure with the permission of Anderson Erickson.

Serves 6 6 grams of fat per serving

- 6 lasagna noodles
- 1 10-ounce package frozen chopped broccoli
- 2 cups Anderson Erickson Skim Milk
- 2 tablespoons cornstarch
- 1 tablespoon minced dried onion
- 1½ cups diced cooked ham
- ½ teaspoon Italian seasoning, crushed
- 1 cup Anderson Erickson Lite Cottage Cheese
- 1 cup shredded mozzarella cheese (4 ounces)

1. Cook the lasagna noodles according to directions on the package; drain. Rinse with cold water.
2. Cook the broccoli according to package directions; drain.
3. To make the sauce, stir together the skim milk, cornstarch, and dried onion in a medium saucepan. Cook and stir until thickened and bubbly; then cook and stir for 2 minutes more.
4. Stir in the cooked broccoli, ham and Italian seasoning.
5. Spread 2 tablespoons of the sauce in bottom of a 10x6x2-inch baking dish.
6. Place two lasagna noodles in baking dish. Spread noodles with half of the cottage cheese. Add one-third of the sauce and mozzarella cheese.
7. Repeat the layers of noodles, cottage cheese, sauce and mozzarella.
8. Top with remaining noodles, sauce, and mozzarella.
9. Bake in a 375° oven for 30-35 minutes or until heated through. Let stand for 10 minutes.

Main Event

There is no more beautiful area in the Midwest than McGregor, located on the Mississippi River in the northeast corner of Iowa. The Mississippi became a major artery as our country developed westward, and hundreds of riverboats steamed up and down the river every year. In 1863 McGregor was the largest port for grain and produce in the country. Much of McGregor has been restored; and several former hotels, originally built to accommodate river travelers, are now private residences. The American House, owned and restored by the Bickels, is one of them.

Bickel's Squirrel Feed for Fifty

John P. Bickel of McGregor has had a long love affair with the riverboats that shaped the history of the Mississippi River. For 25 years he worked toward the establishment of The National Rivers Hall of Fame, now located in the Dubuque Harbor. He is an avid hunter and fisherman who especially loves squirrel hunting, and his annual squirrel dinner for 50 - 100 guests is a local tradition.

Serves 50   Grams of fat not available

30 - 50 squirrels, quartered   **Salt and pepper to taste**
6 - 10 large onions, chopped   **Juniper berries**
Bacon slices, cut in small strips

1. Soak the squirrel in cold, salted water for 10 minutes.
2. Drain the squirrel and place first layer in the bottom of a large roaster.
3. Sprinkle lightly with chopped onions, salt, pepper and a few juniper berries.
4. Place a second layer of squirrel on the onions and repeat the process, adding the bacon strips on alternate layers until all of the squirrel is used..
5. Cover and bake at 450° for 20 minutes. Lower the oven temperature to 300° and bake for an additional 2½ hours.

Vegetables and Side Dishes

Vegetables and Side Dishes

Garden Ratatouille

The roadside stands along Iowa highways overflow with an abundance of produce during harvest season. This combination of vegetables is a good way to enjoy the bounty. Remember to make a double recipe and freeze half; it's wonderful served over pasta or a baked potato for a quick meal. Served hot, cold or at room temperature, it is delicious and has very little fat.

Serves 6   2.2 grams of fat per serving

- 1 tablespoon canola oil
- 2 medium onions, sliced
- 1 medium sweet red pepper, chopped
- 1 tablespoon minced garlic
- 1 small eggplant, cubed
- 3 medium zucchini, cut into ½-inch slices
- ¾ cup canned whole tomatoes, undrained
- 2 tablespoons fresh minced parsley
- 1 teaspoon dried basil
- ½ teaspoon dried oregano
- 2 large tomatoes, skinned and chopped
- ½ teaspoon salt
- Freshly ground black pepper

1. Heat the oil in a large skillet; add the onions, red peppers and garlic; sauté for 3 minutes.
2. Add the eggplant, zucchini, canned tomatoes, parsley, basil and oregano. Simmer for 10 minutes, stirring occasionally.
3. Add remaining ingredients and simmer for another 10 minutes.

Vegetables and Side Dishes

Broiled Parmesan Tomatoes

When tomatoes are broiled briefly they become hot but remain firm, and the heat seems to accentuate the wonderful tomato flavor. This may be a French way of preparing tomatoes, but Iowa cooks have brought it home and love it.

Serves 8   3 grams of fat per serving

4 medium tomatoes
Vegetable cooking spray
Salt and pepper to taste
3 tablespoons dry bread crumbs
2 tablespoons Parmesan cheese
2 tablespoons chopped parsley
½ teaspoon garlic powder
2 teaspoons finely chopped fresh basil
1½ tablespoons olive oil

1. Wash the tomatoes; cut off and discard the tops. Slice the tomatoes in half; coat with vegetable spray. Salt and pepper to taste.
2. Combine the remaining ingredients and sprinkle over the cut surface of the tomatoes.
3. Place on a cookie sheet or broiler pan. Broil for 3 minutes or until the cheese mixture is lightly browned.

♥ Greece and Italy have less coronary heart problems than other European countries although they all have about the same amount of fat in their diets. The difference is that olive oil is the major source of fat found in Greek and Italian cooking. Olive oil is a monounsaturated fat, which is more effective in reducing blood cholesterol levels than saturated or polyunsaturated fat. Other oils with monounsaturated fat are peanut oil and canola oil. Keep this in mind when you purchase cooking oil.

Vegetables and Side Dishes

According to Indian legend, there was once a beautiful maiden named Wapsi who fell in love with a handsome brave named Pinicon. He was the son of the chief of a fierce enemy tribe. Because their love was doomed, the two lovers jumped into the river at the spot of their secret rendezvous. Even today you can hear their voices lamenting their lost love if you listen to the murmur of the Wapsipinicon River. Of course, there are more factual people who say the river's name came from a variety of white artichoke that grew wild along its banks.

Wapsipinicon Tomatoes

Serves 8   *4 grams of fat per serving*

- 6 large tomatoes, peeled
- 2 10-ounce packages frozen chopped spinach, thawed
- 6 green onions, chopped
- 1 clove garlic, minced
- ½ cup egg substitute
- 2 tablespoons melted margarine
- ½ teaspoon Worcestershire sauce
- ¼ teaspoon Tabasco sauce
- ½ teaspoon salt
- ½ cup dry bread crumbs (reserve ¼ cup for topping)
- ¼ cup grated mozzarella or Parmesan cheese

1. Cut each tomato into 3 thick slices. Layer in the bottom of a large, flat baking dish.
2. Squeeze the spinach to remove most of the moisture.
3. Combine with the remaining ingredients, except for the reserved bread crumbs and the cheese.
4. Mound a spoonful of the spinach mixture on top of each slice of tomato.
5. Combine the reserved bread crumbs and cheese and sprinkle over the top of the spinach mixture. Bake at 350° for 20-25 minutes.

Vegetables and Side Dishes

Iowa is called the Corn State and it's here that "the tall corn grows." Would you believe the record corn stalk measured over 31 feet? Driving through Iowa on a summer day, one can see mile after mile of cornfields marching over the gently rolling hills. The long, straight rows of corn of various shades of green, punctuated here and there by neat fences, tell you that this is a lush, orderly place carefully tended by man.

Easy Corn on the Cob

For cooking small batches of corn on the cob, no method is easier than microwaving; and it allows the corn to retain its flavor and crispness. Plan on 2-3 minutes for each ear of corn-less time if corn is very tender, a little more if it's not as fresh. As Iowans will tell you, it's important to get the corn from the field to the table as quickly as possible. Also, buy corn still in the husks because the husks help retain flavor and freshness.

Serves 2   0 grams of fat per serving

**2 large ears of corn,   1 teaspoon water
    husks and silks removed**

1. Place the corn in a microwave-safe dish. Add water and cover with waxed paper or plastic film.
2. Pierce the paper several times and microwave on High for 5 - 6 minutes.
3. Let stand in microwave for 1 minute to complete cooking. Remove waxed paper or plastic wrap carefully to prevent being scalded by the steam.

VARIATION: UNHUSKED CORN ON THE COB: Many corn lovers believe that microwaving corn in the husks brings out more of the natural corn flavor. Just remove any outer husks that are wilted or soiled and follow the above instructions. The silks will pull away easily after cooking.

Vegetables and Side Dishes

Grilled Corn on the Cob

Microwaving the corn before placing it on the grill cuts cooking time and insures the corn will be evenly cooked. If you choose not to microwave the corn first, soak it in water for several minutes and allow 25-30 minutes on the grill.

Serves   5 grams of fat per serving

4 ears corn
2 tablespoons margarine
1 teaspoon chili powder
½ teaspoon onion powder
½ teaspoon salt
Dash of black pepper
2 tablespoons water

1. Pull the husks carefully from the corn so they remain attached to end of the corn ear. Remove silks from the corn.
2. Melt the butter in a small saucepan. Add the seasonings and mix.
3. Brush the seasoned butter on the corn.
4. Replace the corn husks, completely covering the corn, and tie with a string.
5. Sprinkle water over the corn. Microwave on High for 6 minutes.
6. Immediately place the corn directly on the grill over medium-hot coals.
7. Cook, turning frequently, for 10-15 minutes.
8. Remove the seared husks before serving.

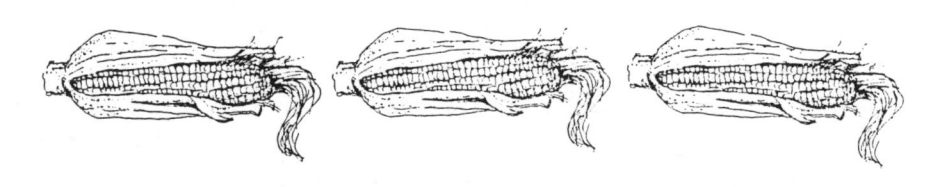

Vegetables and Side Dishes

Vegetable Medley

*My favorite cooking class was one given by Jean Durkee, author of **Tout de Suite a la Microwave I** and **Tout de Suite a la Microwave II**, two best-selling cookbooks featuring gourmet cooking in the microwave oven. With her permission, I'm passing along this beautiful way to serve vegetables from her second book.*

Serves 8   5.5 grams fat per serving

- ½ head cauliflower, cut into flowerets
- ½ bunch broccoli, cut into flowerets
- 1 (12-ounce) bag medium carrots, sliced round or in sticks
- 1 yellow squash, sliced round
- 1 zucchini, sliced round or in sticks
- 2 medium onions, quartered
- 6 whole Brussels sprouts
- 4 large whole mushrooms
- 1 green or red bell pepper, cut in rings
- ¼ cup margarine, melted
- 1-2 teaspoons Morton Nature's Seasons or Jane's Krazy Mixed-up salt

1. Arrange rinsed and prepared vegetables on a 12-inch glass plate in an attractive, colorful way with the harder vegetables (cauliflower, broccoli and carrots) on the outer edge of plate.
2. Place the softer vegetables (squash and zucchini) in the center of plate, with onions, Brussels sprouts and mushrooms midway between the outer and center circles.
3. Place slices of bell pepper on top. Do not season or add water.
4. Cover tightly with thin plastic wrap (will take two sheets). Do not puncture.
5. Microwave on High (100%) for 10 minutes. Check vegetables for doneness (test carrots), remembering to lift wrap away from you.

Vegetables and Side Dishes

6. Cook for an additional 2 minutes for softer vegetables. Cooking time is approximately 5 minutes per pound of vegetables.
7. Drain liquid from vegetables, reserve for soup or gravy, and pour or squeeze margarine over cooked vegetables. Sprinkle with seasoned salt.

Matchstick Zucchini and Carrots

Because the vegetables are cut into julienne strips, they cook quickly and taste especially fresh. Choose the long, firm zucchini - they are usually crisper and have fewer seeds than the chunkier ones.

Serves 6   2.5 grams of fat per serving

2 medium zucchini, unpeeled
4 medium carrots, peeled
Vegetable cooking spray
1 tablespoon olive oil
2 tablespoons chicken broth

1 teaspoon lemon juice
1 teaspoon chopped fresh dill
Salt and pepper (optional)
Fresh dill sprigs

1. Cut the zucchini and carrots lengthwise into slices ¼-inch thick. Stack the slices and cut into ¼-inch strips about 3 inches long. Or use the julienne blade on your food processor or mandolin. Set strips aside.
2. Coat a nonstick skillet with vegetable spray. Add the oil and place over medium heat. Add the carrots and sauté for 1 minute.
3. Add the chicken broth and simmer briefly. Add the zucchini, lemon juice, dill and seasonings. Cover and cook for 3 minutes or until vegetables are tender but still crisp.
4. Salt and pepper to taste. Serve warm, garnished with sprigs of fresh dill.

Vegetables and Side Dishes

The summer of 1993 will be hard for Iowans to forget. The flood that made much of Iowa look like an enormous lake was notable not only because it was so much worse than any recorded before but because it refused to go away. The rains of the summer followed the rains of the spring, and the waterlogged soil and swollen streams were deluged with still more rain. The constant downpours and flooding rivers tested the patience, courage and humor of thousands of Iowans and left the rest of the country in awe of their ability to cope with overwhelming problems.

Ames Vegetable Casserole

Edna Tegtmeier of Ames shares this recipe for an easy-to-put-together casserole of mixed vegetables that can be prepared the day before and refrigerated. She says she has found that it freezes well.

Serves 8   7 grams of fat

- 2½ cups green beans, drained
- 2 cups sliced carrots
- 2 cups chopped celery
- 1½ sliced onion, cut into strips
- 1 tablespoon sugar
- ¼ teaspoon pepper
- 3 tablespoons Minute Tapioca
- 4 tablespoons melted margarine
- 3½ cups canned stewed tomatoes

1. Combine all the ingredients in a 3-quart casserole.
2. Cover the casserole and bake at 350° for 1½ hours, stirring occasionally.

Vegetables and Side Dishes

Dor's Spinach-Broccoli Bake

Smart, talented Dorothea Sidney of Des Moines shares this vegetable casserole that bakes so light it is almost a soufflé.

Serves 4   9.5 grams of fat per serving

- 1 10-ounce box frozen chopped broccoli
- 1 10-ounce box frozen chopped spinach
- 2 tablespoons flour
- 1 12-ounce carton low-fat cottage cheese
- ½ cup egg substitute
- 1½ cups shredded sharp Cheddar cheese
- Salt to taste
- Vegetable cooking spray
- ½ cup dry bread crumbs
- 2 teaspoons melted margarine

1. Thaw the broccoli and spinach. Squeeze to remove almost all the moisture.
2. Combine the broccoli and spinach with the flour, cottage cheese, egg substitute, cheese and salt.
3. Coat a 6-cup baking dish with cooking spray. Turn the broccoli-spinach mixture into the dish.
4. Combine the bread crumbs with the melted margarine and sprinkle on top. Bake for 1 hour at 350°.

Vegetables and Side Dishes

Jean's Beans

Beans with ham hocks were one of those old family dishes we considered a "comfort" food. Beans, with their high-fiber content and no fat or cholesterol are wonderful for a low-fat diet; but the ham hocks had to go. We found that smoked pork chops, with only 3 grams of fat each, added a lot of flavor and very little fat.

Serves 6   *2 grams of fat per serving*

- 1 pound Great Northern dried beans
- 1 medium onion, minced
- 2 cloves garlic, minced
- 2 carrots, sliced
- ½ cup chopped celery
- ½ teaspoon black pepper
- 3 smoked pork chops, trimmed and cubed
- 2 teaspoons salt
- 1 teaspoon brown sugar
- 1 tablespoon prepared mustard

1. Wash the beans and place in a large kettle with 2 quarts water. Let soak for 3-4 hours or overnight.
2. Drain the beans and cover with fresh water.
3. Add the onion, garlic, carrots and celery.
4. Cover and simmer slowly for 2 hours stirring occasionally. Check the water level in the kettle, adding more as needed.
5. Add the remaining ingredients and simmer for another hour or until tender.

Vegetables and Side Dishes

Creamy Baked Onions

Onions are a wonderful vegetable, but are usually used to add flavor instead of standing on their own. This side dish is especially good when served with either beef or pork.

Serves 6   4.2 grams of fat per serving

- 4 large sweet onions
- 2 tablespoons margarine
- 2 cloves garlic, minced
- ¼ cup chicken broth
- 1 10¾-ounce can cream of chicken fat-free soup
- ¼ cup grated Parmesan cheese
- 2 teaspoons sodium-reduced soy sauce
- ½ teaspoon black pepper
- ½ cup seasoned bread crumbs

1. Peel and slice the onions. Separate into rings.
2. Reserve 1 tablespoon of margarine for the topping. Place 1 tablespoon of margarine, the garlic and the chicken broth in a large saucepan. Add the onions rings and simmer until tender.
3. Transfer the onion rings and broth to a 2-quart casserole.
4. Mix the soup, Parmesan cheese, soy sauce, and pepper and pour over the onions.
5. Melt the reserved margarine and mix with the bread crumbs.
6. Sprinkle the bread crumb mixture over the top of the onion mixture and bake at 350° for 30 minutes.

Vegetables and Side Dishes

New Potatoes with Mushrooms

Serves 8   2 grams of fat per serving

- 20 small new potatoes, scrubbed
- 2 cups fresh mushrooms
- 1 tablespoon olive oil
- 1 large clove garlic, finely minced
- 2 tablespoons chopped fresh parsley
- 2 tablespoons chopped fresh chives
- 1 tablespoon chopped fresh basil
- Salt and pepper to taste

1. Peel a narrow strip around each potato. Cut any larger potatoes in half.
2. Wipe the mushrooms and trim ends of the stems. If the mushrooms are large, cut them in half.
3. Toss the potatoes with the mushrooms, oil and garlic in a medium-sized bowl using your hands to coat evenly. Mix in the herbs, salt and pepper.
3. Place the mixture in a 3-quart baking dish. Bake at 350° for 45 minutes or until potatoes are tender.

Low-Fat Scalloped Potatoes

Serves 4-6   3 grams of fat per serving

- 6 medium potatoes, sliced ¼-inch thick
- Salt and pepper to taste
- 2 tablespoons minced onion
- ⅓ cup Cream Sauce Base (page 115)
- 1¼ cups water
- ¼ cup grated Cheddar cheese
- 2 tablespoons bread crumbs

1. Place half of the potatoes in a small casserole; add salt, pepper and half of the onion.
2. Mix the Cream Sauce Base with the water and microwave on High for 4 minutes, stirring after 2 minutes. Cream Sauce should be thickened.

Vegetables and Side Dishes

3. Pour half of the sauce over the potatoes in the casserole. Sprinkle half of the grated cheese over the sauce.
4. Repeat the process with the remaining potatoes, onion and sauce.
5. Mix the bread crumbs with the rest of the cheese and sprinkle on top.
6. Cover casserole and bake at 350° for 40 minutes. Remove cover and bake for another 30 minutes or until the potatoes are tender.

Sliced Oven-Roasted Potatoes

Serves 4   5 grams of fat per serving

4 medium-sized baking potatoes, unpeeled
Vegetable cooking spray
½ teaspoon Knorr's Seasoning
2 teaspoons dried parsley
1 tablespoon margarine, melted
2 tablespoons grated Parmesan cheese

1. Scrub the potatoes and slice ¼-inch thick.
2. Coat a glass baking dish with cooking spray. Place the potato slices so they overlap each other about half the width of the slice.
3. Sprinkle the slices with the Knorr's Seasoning and dried parsley. Drizzle with the margarine.
4. Bake at 425° for 45 minutes.
5. Remove from the oven and sprinkle with the Parmesan cheese. Return to the oven and bake for another 10 minutes.

Vegetables and Side Dishes

Not-To-Worry Fried Potatoes

My husband loves fried potatoes and did not want to give them up when we started low-fat cooking. After several experiments, he gave these his stamp of approval. They have the taste and the crunch you want in fried potatoes, but little fat.

Serves 4   7 grams of fat per serving

4 or 5 medium potatoes, cooked and cooled
2 tablespoons oil
½ cup finely chopped onion
½ teaspoon dried rosemary
1 teaspoon salt
½ teaspoon black pepper
Vegetable cooking spray

1. Slice the potatoes into a large bowl. Add ½ tablespoon oil, chopped onion, dried rosemary, salt and pepper. Toss to mix thoroughly.
2. Coat a large nonstick skillet with cooking spray. Heat the remaining oil and add the potatoes. Cook over moderately high heat, turning as they brown.
3. Cook for 10-12 minutes or until potatoes and onions are nicely browned.

> ♥ Nonstick skillets or frying pans reduce the fat needed when browning food. If you also use a cooking spray, you can often eliminate the need for oil altogether.

Vegetables and Side Dishes

Stuffed Baked Potato

This is all you need for an easy lunch or a light supper. If you haven't much time, cook the potatoes in the microwave 6-8 minutes for one potato and another 3-4 minutes for each additional potato. Be sure to pierce them with a fork so they don't explode in the microwave. To make the potatoes more like oven-baked, wrap them in a damp paper towel before putting in the microwave. Let them stand in the microwave for 3 minutes after cooking. The time needed to bake the potatoes will vary according to the size of the potatoes.

Serves 4   1 gram of fat per serving

- 4 medium-large baking potatoes
- ½ cup chopped onion
- ½ cup chopped green pepper
- 2 cloves garlic, minced
- Vegetable cooking spray
- 1 teaspoon olive oil
- 1 teaspoon fresh basil
- ½ teaspoon salt
- ½ teaspoon black pepper
- 1 14½-ounce can stewed tomatoes

1. Wash the potatoes; pierce with a fork and microwave for 16-20 minutes, or bake for 1 hour in a 400° oven. Poke with a fork to determine if they are done as the time will vary depending on size.

2. While the potatoes are baking, coat a large nonstick skillet with cooking spray and place over medium heat. Add the oil and sauté the onion, green pepper and garlic for 3 minutes. Add the seasoning and stewed tomatoes; simmer for another 5 minutes.

3. When the potatoes are done, cut them halfway through from side to side and again from top to bottom. Push the ends of the potato towards each other until the potato opens. Ladle the sauce over the potatoes and serve.

Vegetables and Side Dishes

Country Potatoes

The green peppers, tomatoes and mushrooms combine with the potatoes to make a delicious and attractive dish that can be prepared ahead of time.

Serves 8　　　　　6.5 grams fat per serving

- 8 large potatoes, cooked
- Vegetable cooking spray
- 1 tablespoon margarine
- 1 green pepper, chopped
- 1 medium onion, chopped
- 1 cup stewed tomatoes
- 1 3-ounce can sliced mushrooms
- Salt and pepper to taste
- ½ cup shredded sharp Cheddar cheese

1. Cut the cooked, unpeeled potatoes into ¾-inch chunks and place in a 2-quart casserole.
2. Coat a nonstick skillet with cooking spray. Add the margarine and melt over medium heat. Add the green pepper and onion and sauté until transparent. Spread over the potatoes.
3. Add the tomatoes, mushrooms and seasonings, mixing gently.
4. Top with the shredded cheese, cover with aluminum foil and bake at 350° for 25 minutes.
5. Remove the foil and bake for another 20 minutes or until potatoes and cheese are lightly browned.

> ♥ There are 9 grams of fat in 1 ounce of Cheddar cheese, so use cheese carefully. No doubt a new lot-fat cheese that is acceptable to cheese lovers will appear soon. Till then, it's better to cut the amount of cheese used in a recipe.

Vegetables and Side Dishes

Roasted Root Vegetables

This recipe comes from Jo Freeman of Des Moines, and it is one of her favorite ways to serve vegetables for winter dinner parties. The ingredients can be varied according to what is available in your local market.

Serves 8   5.5 grams of fat per serving

- 2-3 pounds root vegetables, carrots, potatoes, onions, parsnips, rutabagas, turnips, etc.
- 4 tablespoons margarine
- ½ cup chicken stock (more if needed)
- Salt and freshly ground black pepper
- 2 tablespoons chopped fresh herbs, thyme, oregano, parsley, dill, etc.

1. Preheat the oven to 375°.
2. Scrub or peel the vegetables; cut into 2-inch pieces.
3. Place the margarine and chicken stock in a shallow roasting pan and heat until margarine is melted.
4. Add the vegetables, turn and stir until thoroughly coated. Add salt and pepper to taste.
5. Roast uncovered for 1½ hours, stirring several times. Add more chicken stock if necessary to keep vegetables moist.
6. Sprinkle the herbs over the vegetables and mix; transfer the vegetables to a warm serving plate.

Vegetables and Side Dishes

Baked Wild Rice with Herbs

Wild rice is a delicacy grown in the lakes of Minnesota, the state that borders Iowa to the north. It is expensive, but its distinctive flavor is a wonderful accompaniment to poultry or pork. The best wild rice is the long-grain, premium-quality type that is so dark it's almost black.

Serves 8   7 grams of fat per serving

- 1 cup uncooked wild rice
- ¼ cup margarine
- 1 cup chopped celery
- 1 cup chopped onion or leeks
- ½ cup sliced mushrooms
- 4-5 cups chicken broth
- 1 tablespoon chopped fresh parsley
- ¼ teaspoon thyme
- ¼ teaspoon dried basil or 1 teaspoon fresh basil
- ½ teaspoon salt
- ½ teaspoon black pepper

1. Rinse the wild rice carefully and let soak while preparing the other ingredients.
2. Melt the margarine in a large skillet over medium heat. Add the celery, onion or leeks and the mushrooms. Stir until the vegetables are translucent.
3. Drain the wild rice and add to the skillet; cook and stir for 2 minutes. Place wild rice mixture in a 2-quart baking dish.
4. Stir in 4 cups of the chicken broth and the herbs and seasonings.
5. Cover and bake in a 350° over for 1½ hours, stirring occasionally. Add more broth the last 20 minutes if needed.

Sweets and Treats

Sweets and Treats

Iowans have long cherished the covered bridges of Madison County. They were built to give protection from ice and snow, but they also sheltered travelers during rainstorms, served as billboards for local merchants and were used as churches by early circuit-riding preachers. With the popularity of James Waller's best-selling novel, *The Bridges of Madison County*, existence of the bridges has become known far and wide.

Madison County Apple Crisp

Millions of apple trees have come from the stock of one seedling that grew in Madison County in the orchard of Amos Hiatt. Everyone who tasted his apples pronounced them "delicious," and from that tree the Delicious apple was developed. This simple, satisfying dessert is especially good when served while still warm from the oven.

Serves 7   4.7 grams of fat per serving

- 6 - 7 tart apples, pared and sliced
- 1 tablespoon lemon juice
- ¼ cup sugar
- Pinch of salt
- 1 teaspoon cinnamon
- 1 cup quick-cooking oats
- ⅓ cup brown sugar
- ½ cup flour
- 3 tablespoons margarine, melted

1. Spread the apple slices in a 9x9-inch baking pan and sprinkle with the lemon juice, sugar, salt and cinnamon.
2. Combine the oats, brown sugar, flour and margarine and spread over the apple filling.
3. Bake at 350° for 35-40 minutes or until the fruit is bubbly and the topping is lightly browned.

Sweets and Treats

Peach-Blueberry Crisp

Serves 8   5 grams of fat per serving

- 6 cups peeled and sliced fresh peaches
- 2 cups fresh blueberries
- 2 teaspoons lemon juice
- 1 teaspoon almond extract

- ⅓ cup brown sugar, packed
- 2 tablespoons all-purpose flour
- 1 teaspoon cinnamon

TOPPING:
- 1 cup quick-cooking rolled oats
- 1 teaspoon cinnamon

- ¼ cup brown sugar, packed
- 3 tablespoons melted butter

1. Place the peaches, blueberries, lemon juice and almond extract in a medium bowl. Combine the sugar, flour and cinnamon; add to fruit and mix.
2. Turn the mixture into a 9x9-inch baking dish.
3. Make the topping by combining the oats, cinnamon, brown sugar and melted margarine.
4. Sprinkle over the top of the fruit mixture. Bake in 375° oven for 25 minutes or until the top is golden brown and the fruit is bubbly. Serve warm or cold.

Sweets and Treats

Summer Peach Trifle

*When this was recently served as the finale of a special party, **everyone** wanted the recipe. You can substitute fresh berries for the peaches and have a berry trifle that is equally good. The trifle is best if made the day ahead.*

Serves 10   6 grams of fat per serving

- 1 3-ounce box vanilla pudding made with 1¾ cups skim milk
- 1 16-ounce Free & Light Sara Lee Pound Cake
- ½ cup orange juice
- 8-10 large ripe peaches
- 2 tablespoons lemon juice
- 3 tablespoons honey
- ½ cup apricot jam
- ½ teaspoon almond flavoring
- 1 12-ounce tub non-dairy whipped topping
- 5 sprigs fresh mint

1. Cook the vanilla pudding and set aside to cool.
2. Cut the pound cake into 1-inch slices. Place half of the slices in the bottom of a deep 8-inch glass bowl or trifle dish.
3. Pour half of the orange juice over the cake in the bowl.
4. Peel and slice the peaches and sprinkle with lemon juice. Reserve a few slices for garnish.
5. Microwave the honey and jam for 40 seconds to liquefy. Add the almond flavoring and combine with the peaches.
6. Layer half of the peach mixture over the cake in the bowl.
7. Mix the cooled vanilla pudding with half of the whipped topping.
8. Spread half of the vanilla pudding mix over the top of the peaches in the bowl.
9. Repeat the layering process, finishing with the reserved whipped topping. Garnish with the reserved peach slices and sprigs of fresh mint.

Sweets and Treats

Patty's Frozen Strawberry Dessert

Patty Crispin, a dear friend who lives in Tingley, dictated this delicious dessert recipe to me over the phone. The pecan and strawberry flavors combine beautifully for a light, smooth frozen dessert.

Serves 12   11.5 grams of fat per serving

CRUST:
- 1 cup flour
- ¼ cup brown sugar
- ½ cup margarine
- ½ cup chopped pecans

1. Mix the crust ingredients thoroughly and press evenly in the bottom of a 9x13-inch baking dish.
2. Bake at 350° for 12-15 minutes.
3. Allow crust to cool; stir to crumble crust. Reserve ½ cup of crumbs for topping. Sprinkle the remaining crumbs in the bottom of the baking dish.

FILLING:
- 2 egg whites
- ½ cup sugar
- 1 teaspoon lemon juice
- 2½ cups frozen strawberries with juice, thawed
- 1½ cups non-dairy whipped topping

1. Beat the egg whites until frothy and add the sugar. Continue beating for about 5 minutes or until stiff.
2. Add the lemon juice and thawed strawberries; beat until thick and creamy.
3. Fold in the non-dairy whipped topping.
4. Spread the filling over the crust crumbs. Sprinkle the reserved crumbs over the top of the filling. Freeze for at least 3 hours or until firm.

Sweets and Treats

Iowa's gently rolling countryside is a surprise to many who visualize Iowa as a flat, unbroken landscape. When Hollywood movie men were searching for a large area of level farm land as the location for a movie, they had to go next door to Illinois to find what they were looking for. Iowa is named for the Ioway Indians and it is thought the word Ioway means "beautiful land."

Strawberry-Rhubarb Crunch

For a few weeks in the spring, rhubarb and strawberries are available at the same time. Seize the moment to combine these two flavors that go so well together.

Serves 8   5.4 grams of fat per serving

- 4 cups sliced rhubarb
- 1 cup strawberries, hulled and halved
- ¾ cup sugar
- 2 tablespoons cornstarch
- ½ tablespoon egg substitute
- 1 teaspoon grated orange rind
- ⅓ cup quick-cooking oats
- ⅓ cup all-purpose flour
- ½ teaspoon cinnamon
- 3 tablespoons margarine, melted

1. Combine the rhubarb, strawberries, sugar, cornstarch, egg substitute and grated orange rind in a large mixing bowl. Let the mixture stand for 20 minutes, stirring occasionally.
2. Turn the mixture into a 9x9-inch baking dish.
3. Combine the oats, flour and cinnamon in a small mixing bowl. Mix in the margarine until well blended.
4. Sprinkle the oat mixture over the top of the rhubarb mixture.
5. Bake for 40-45 minutes at 350° or until the topping is lightly browned and the rhubarb mixture is bubbly.

Sweets and Treats

Harvest Pumpkin Pie

Harvest season in Iowa and pumpkin pie go together, so here's a pie that you can eat without guilt. The pie tastes every bit as good as the one made with eggs and high-fat evaporated milk.

Serves 8   5 grams of fat per serving

- 1½ cups graham cracker crumbs
- 2 tablespoons melted margarine
- 1 16-ounce can pumpkin
- ½ cup egg substitute
- ½ cup brown sugar
- ½ teaspoon salt
- 1 teaspoon cinnamon
- ½ teaspoon nutmeg
- ¼ teaspoon ground cloves
- ½ teaspoon vanilla
- 1 12-ounce can evaporated skimmed milk

1. Place the graham cracker crumbs in a medium bowl. Pour the margarine over crumbs and mix well.
2. Press the mixture onto the bottom and sides of a 9-inch pie pan.
3. Combine the pumpkin, egg substitute, brown sugar, spices and vanilla in a large mixing bowl. Blend in the evaporated milk.
4. Pour the pumpkin mixture into the graham cracker crust and bake at 375° for 55-60 minutes or until a knife inserted near the center of the pie comes out clean.

Sweets and Treats

Drake University Slice-O-Lemon Pie

The recipe for this unusual double-crust lemon pie comes from Jeanette Harmon Baker, who remembers it from Drake functions when her father was President of Drake University. The lemon slices add a delicious burst of tartness to the custard filling. It's a wonderful dessert, but not low-fat; so if you splurge, keep the rest of your day's intake to very low-fat food.

Serves 7   25.2 grams of fat per serving

- 2 unbaked 8-inch pie crusts
- 1¼ cups sugar
- 2 tablespoons flour
- ⅛ teaspoon salt
- ¼ cup soft butter or margarine
- 3 eggs (reserve 1 teaspoon egg white for crust)
- 1 teaspoon grated lemon rind
- 1 medium lemon, peeled and sliced-paper thin
- ½ cup water
- Pinch of cinnamon and sugar, mixed

1. Fit one pie crust into an 8-inch pie pan. Reserve the other crust for the top of the pie.
2. Combine the sugar, flour and salt in a medium bowl. Blend the butter or margarine into the sugar mixture.
3. Beat the eggs well, reserving 1 teaspoon egg white for the top crust, and stir into the sugar mixture.
4. Add the grated lemon rind, lemon slices and water, mixing gently until blended. Pour into the pastry-lined pan. Cover with the second crust.
5. Trim any excess pastry, seal and flute edges. Brush the top with the reserved egg white and sprinkle with sugar and cinnamon.
6. Cut slits for steam to escape. Bake for 30-35 minutes at 400°.

Sweets and Treats

Grapefruit Pie

This recipe comes from Lois Clark, one of Burlington's great cooks. She says, "people turn up their noses at the mention of Grapefruit Pie; but when they try it, they all love it." This unusual dessert is pretty and has a tart, refreshing flavor. The only fat is in the crust; so if you want to trim the fat content, just leave those last few bites of crust uneaten.

Serves 7   8 grams of fat per serving

1 9-inch pie crust
3 large pink grapefruit
1 cup sugar (a little less if grapefruit is sweet)

1 cup water
2 tablespoons cornstarch
3 tablespoons strawberry gelatin
Non-dairy whipped topping

1. Prepare the pie crust and bake until golden brown.
2. Use a sharp knife to peel the grapefruit, removing all the white pith. Cut out each section so it is free of any membrane.
3. Drain the grapefruit on paper towels and pat dry.
4. Place the grapefruit sections in the baked pie crust.
5. Cook the sugar, water and cornstarch over medium heat until mixture thickens.
6. Remove from heat, add the gelatin and stir until dissolved.
7. Cool slightly, pour over the grapefruit and chill.
8. Decorate with the topping.

Sweets and Treats

Chocolate-Banana Bread Pudding

Early Iowa housewives used day-old bread to make bread pudding and it became a favorite dessert of many families. This updated version is delicious, quick and easy to make and has very little fat per serving.

Serves 8   *1 gram of fat per serving*

8 slices firm white bread
Vegetable cooking spray
4 tablespoons cocoa
4 tablespoons sugar
3 ripe bananas, mashed
4 tablespoons non-fat dry milk
2 egg whites
¼ teaspoon salt
1 cup skim milk
1 teaspoon vanilla
Frozen non-fat vanilla yogurt

1. Preheat the oven to 325°.
2. Cut the bread into 1-inch cubes. Toast about 15 minutes or until lightly browned.
3. Spray a 9x9-inch baking dish with cooking spray. Spread the bread cubes evenly on the bottom of the dish. Set aside.
4. Combine the cocoa, sugar, bananas, non-fat dry milk, egg whites, salt, skim milk and vanilla in a blender or food processor and blend until smooth.
5. Pour over the toasted bread cubes, making sure all sides are coated.
6. Bake for 25 minutes or until firm.
7. Remove from heat and allow to cool slightly. Top with non-fat frozen yogurt and serve while still warm.

Sweets and Treats

Pella is known for the tulips that provide a dazzling display each spring. Its streets and sidewalks are lined with thousands and thousands wonderful blooms. The town was settle by people of Dutch heritage, and the townspeople have been effective in preserving the culture, crafts and cooking of their native Holland.

Chocolate Roll

This is an elegant dessert to make for special occasions, and it's our family's favorite for Christmas dinner.

Serves 10   12 grams of fat per serving

ROLL:
- 6 egg whites
- ½ teaspoon cream of tartar
- 1 cup sugar
- 6 egg yolks
- 4 tablespoons cocoa
- 4 tablespoons flour
- ½ teaspoon salt
- 1 teaspoon vanilla

1. Beat the egg whites and cream of tartar until stiff. Gradually add ½ cup sugar (reserve ½ cup) and beat until glossy. Set aside.
2. Beat the yolks until thick; beat in reserved ½ cup sugar.
3. Sift the dry ingredients together and stir into the yolk mixture. Mix in vanilla.
4. Gently fold into the beaten egg whites and spread the mixture in a 10x15-inch pan lined with waxed paper coated with cooking spray. Bake at 325° for 25 minutes or until cake springs back when lightly touched.
6. Turn upside down on a tea towel that has been lightly sprinkled with powdered sugar. Immediately remove the waxed paper and roll lengthwise with the towel. Let cool.

Sweets and Treats

FILLING:
- ½ teaspoon gelatin
- ½ tablespoon warm low-fat milk
- 8-ounces non-dairy whipped topping

1. Soften gelatin in warm milk and fold gently into non-dairy whipped topping.
2. Gently unroll the chocolate sponge roll and spread with the filling.
3. Roll back up, removing any excess filling with a rubber spatula.
4. Spread with the Chocolate Gloss.

CHOCOLATE GLOSS:
- ½ cup sugar
- 1½ tablespoons cornstarch
- ¼ teaspoon salt
- 1 1-ounce square unsweetened chocolate
- ½ cup boiling water
- 1 tablespoon margarine
- ½ teaspoon vanilla

1. Mix the sugar, cornstarch, salt, chocolate and boiling water in a small saucepan. Cook and stir over medium heat until the mixture thickens.
2. Remove from the heat. Add the margarine and vanilla
3. Immediately spread over the chocolate roll. When cool, decorate as desired.

Sweets and Treats

Laura's Chocolate Cake

This is a rich, moist cake that tastes delicious. It uses cocoa, which has only 3 grams of fat in ¼ cup, instead of 2 ounces of unsweetened baking chocolate which has 30 grams of fat. Also, substituting buttermilk for some of the oil helps lower the fat content. Make the frosting as soon as the cake comes out of the oven so the cake is still warm when you spread the frosting.

Yields 18 servings   13 grams of fat per serving

- 2 cups sugar
- 2 cups unbleached flour
- 1 teaspoon soda
- 1 teaspoon cinnamon
- 1 cup water
- ½ cup margarine

- ½ cup vegetable oil
- ¼ cup cocoa
- ½ cup buttermilk
- ½ cup egg substitute
- 1 teaspoon vanilla

1. Sift the sugar, flour, soda and cinnamon together into a large mixing bowl. Set aside.
2. Combine the water, margarine, oil and cocoa in a small saucepan and bring to a boil, stirring constantly.
3. Pour over the dry ingredients and mix well.
4. Combine the buttermilk, egg substitute and vanilla and stir into the batter.
5. Pour the batter into a greased and floured 9x13-inch cake pan
6. Bake at 375° for 25-30 minutes.

Sweets and Treats

CHOCOLATE-MOCHA FROSTING:
- 4 tablespoons margarine
- 3 tablespoons cocoa
- 2 tablespoons strong coffee
- 2 cups sifted powdered sugar
- ½ teaspoon vanilla

1. Combine the margarine, cocoa and coffee in a small saucepan and place over medium heat. Bring to a boil, stirring constantly.
2. Remove from heat. Mix in 1½ cup powdered sugar until smooth. Add remaining powdered sugar gradually until frosting is of spreading consistency. Add a few drops of water if frosting becomes thicker than you like.
3. Add the vanilla, mix well and spread on the cake while it is still warm.

Sweets and Treats

Glazed Lemon Bundt Cake

This recipe was converted from one found on a box of Duncan Hines cake mix. The tartness of the lemon rind gives the glaze a nice contrast to the sweetness of the cake. Everyone raves about the cake and it is certainly easy to make.

Serves 1   8 grams of fat per serving

- 1 box Duncan Hines Lemon Supreme Cake Mix
- 1 3.4-ounce box lemon instant pudding mix
- ⅓ cup canola oil
- 1 cup water
- 1 cup egg substitute

1. Preheat the oven to 350°.
2. Stir the cake ingredients in a large bowl. Blend, using an electric mixer for 2 minutes at medium speed.
3. Pour the mixture into a bundt pan that has been coated generously with cooking spray and dusted with flour.
4. Bake for 50 minutes or until toothpick inserted in the center comes out clean.
5. Cool for 30 minutes. Invert pan and carefully remove the cake from the pan.
6. Make Lemon Glaze from the recipe below and spread while the cake is slightly warm.

LEMON GLAZE:
- 1½ tablespoons lemon juice
- 1 teaspoon grated lemon rind
- ¾ cup sifted powdered sugar

1. Combine the ingredients and mix until smooth.
2. Spoon the glaze over the top of the cake, letting it run down the sides. This mixture will be thinner than a frosting.

Sweets and Treats

Date-Nut Bars

A perfect dessert for an Iowa picnic; these moist, flavorful little bars will be a hit with anyone who loves dates.

Yields 24 bars   3 grams of fat per bar

- ¼ cup margarine
- 1 cup brown sugar
- ½ cup egg substitute
- 6 ounces dates, chopped
- ¼ cup pecans, chopped
- ½ cup flour
- ¼ teaspoon salt
- 1 teaspoon baking powder
- ½ teaspoon vanilla
- ½ cup powdered sugar

1. Melt the margarine in a small saucepan. Add the brown sugar and stir over medium heat until blended. Let mixture cool slightly.
2. Stir in the egg substitute, dates and pecans.
3. Combine the flour, salt and baking powder and add to the sugar mixture.
4. Stir in the vanilla.
5. Spread the date mixture in an 8x8-inch baking pan that has been lightly coated with cooking spray.
6. Bake at 350° for 30-35 minutes.
7. Cool in the pan. Cut into 24 bars. Sieve the powdered sugar onto a plate and roll each bar in it to coat. Tap gently to remove any excess so bars are lightly dusted.

Sweets and Treats

Iowa's black soil probably has greater value than all the silver and gold mines in the entire world according to the World Book Encyclopedia. When the glaciers moved across what is now the state of Iowa, they left rich soil measuring several feet deep in some areas. Iowa has one-fourth of the rich black soil that is rated premium in the United States. It's no wonder that Iowa is often called America's "breadbasket."

Date Dreams

These cookies are from an old recipe that required no changing to fit our low-fat criteria. They are unusual and always bring comments and compliments.

Yields 5 dozen cookies

1.5 grams of fat per cookie

1 pound dates (about 3 cups), finely chopped
¾ cup sugar
½ cup flour
½ teaspoon baking powder

¼ teaspoon salt
1 cup chopped pecans, toasted
½ teaspoon vanilla
3 egg whites, stiffly beaten

1. Combine the dates, dry ingredients and pecans in a large bowl.
2. Add the vanilla to the stiffly beaten egg whites and combine with the date mixture.
3. Drop by teaspoonful onto a greased cookie sheet, allowing room for them to double in size.
4. Bake at 325° for 15 minutes.

Sweets and Treats

RAGBRAI is a six-day bicycle ride across Iowa by 7,500 bikers of all ages and physical abilities. It started in 1974 when two columnists for *The Des Moines Register* decided that a good way to find out what Iowa was really like would be to bicycle across the state, stopping in small towns along the way. They casually invited anyone who wanted to come along and were amazed when 300 people showed up. Now more than 10,000 people apply for a chance to be part of RAGBRAI every year. The small towns along the route outdo each other with cookies, lemonade and Iowa hospitality.

Quick No-Bake Cookies

This cookie recipe came from a friend who says she never has time to bake. The cookies take only minutes to prepare and are delicious.

Yields 4 dozen cookies   1.5 grams of fat per cookie

2 cups sugar
6 tablespoons cocoa
½ cup skim milk

1 tablespoon margarine
½ cup peanut butter
3 cups 1-minute oatmeal

1. Mix the sugar and cocoa in a large saucepan. Add the milk gradually and stir until the cocoa is moistened.
2. Bring to a boil over medium heat. Remove and add the margarine, peanut butter and oatmeal. Mix thoroughly.
3. Drop by teaspoon on wax paper and let cool. These keep well when stored in an airtight container in the refrigerator.

Sweets and Treats

Microwave Pecan Brittle

I had never made candy in a microwave oven until a friend called to give me this easy and almost-foolproof recipe. She said it was so good she had just made three batches to share with friends and neighbors. The pecans, with 74 grams of fat per cup, keep it from being low-fat, but they are essential to the recipe. Make it, but try to limit the amount you eat.

Yields 24 pieces 6.5 grams of fat per piece

- 1 cup white sugar
- ½ cup light corn syrup
- 1¾ cups chopped pecans
- 2 tablespoons margarine
- 1 teaspoon vanilla
- 1 heaping teaspoon soda

1. Combine the sugar and the syrup in a 2-quart microwave-safe bowl. Mix well.
2. Microwave on High for 4 minutes.
3. Remove from microwave. Add the nuts and mix thoroughly (the mixture will seem stiff).
4. Microwave on High for another 4 minutes.
5. Remove from microwave. Add the margarine and vanilla and mix.
6. Microwave on High for another 2 minutes.
7. Add the soda and stir. Quickly pour onto a large cookie sheet, spreading as thinly as possible with a spatula and a large spoon.
8. Let cool. Break into pieces.

House Specialties

House Specialties

The Amana Colonies, just west of Iowa City, are a combination of old Amish traditions and new ways of doing things. A visit to the seven villages that make up the Colonies gives a glimpse of rural life as it used to be. Tidy 100-year old houses, family-style German restaurants, antique shops and smokehouses filled with hams and sausages mix with the modern factories producing fine furniture, woolens and major appliances.

Stove-Top Apple Butter

Yield 7 cups   0 grams of fat per serving

- 12 large Granny Smith apples
- 1 cup frozen apple juice concentrate
- 2 tablespoons lemon juice
- 1 cup brown sugar
- 1½ teaspoons cinnamon
- ¼ teaspoon salt
- ¼ teaspoon allspice
- Dash of ground cloves

1. Peel, core and slice the apples into a large, heavy kettle. Add the apple juice concentrate.
2. Place the kettle over medium heat and bring the mixture to a boil.
3. Reduce the heat and simmer for 20 minutes or until the apples are tender.
4. Place the hot mixture in a food processor or blender and pureé briefly. Leave some small chunks to add to the texture. Return the apple mixture to the kettle.
5. Stir in the remaining ingredients and cook, stirring often, over low heat for about 30 minutes or until mixture thickens. Watch carefully as the mixture will scorch easily as it begins to thicken.

House Specialties

Pickled Beets

Yields 1 quart   0 grams of fat per serving

- 2 16-ounce cans sliced beets
- 1 cup cider vinegar
- ¾ cup brown sugar
- 1 teaspoon whole allspice
- 10 whole cloves
- 1 2-inch piece of stick cinnamon

1. Drain the beets, reserving the juice.
2. Combine the beet juice with the remaining ingredients in a medium saucepan. Bring to a boil over medium heat.
3. Spoon the beets into 2 clean pint jars and pour the juice mixture over them.
4. Seal the jars and refrigerate for several days for flavors to blend.

Pickled Peaches

Yields 2 pints   0 grams of fat per serving

- 1 cup cider vinegar
- 1 cup water
- 2 cups sugar
- 1 teaspoon ground cloves
- 1 quart peaches, peeled
- 6 whole cloves
- 2 cinnamon sticks

1. Combine the vinegar, water, sugar and ground cloves in a stainless steel or enamel pan and boil for 10 minutes.
2. Add the peaches to the syrup and cook for 20-25 minutes or until tender.
3. Pack the peaches in 2 sterilized pint jars. Add 3 whole cloves and a cinnamon stick to each jar. Cover the peaches with syrup.
4. Seal immediately. Allow at least 2 weeks before serving.

House Specialties

Cranberry-Orange Relish

The grated orange peel adds a tang that perks up the traditional cranberry sauce often served with chicken or turkey. This will keep several days if refrigerated.

Yields 1 quart   8 grams of fat per serving

3 cups fresh cranberries
1 teaspoon grated orange peel
1 large orange
¾ cup orange juice

1½ cups sugar
½ teaspoon nutmeg
½ teaspoon cinnamon
2 tablespoons Grand Marnier liqueur (optional)

1. Wash the cranberries and discard any stems.
2. Grate the orange peel. Peel, seed and chop the orange.
3. Combine all the ingredients, except liqueur, in a large saucepan. Bring to a boil over medium heat, stirring occasionally.
4. Reduce heat, simmer and stir for 10 minutes.
5. Stir in the liqueur. Chill for several hours before serving.

House Specialties

Herb Seasoning Mix

Making your own seasoning mix lets you flavor your cooking to your own taste. This mix is made with dried herbs and spices. If you use fresh herbs in cooking you will need to triple the amount called for.

Yields ¼ cup   0 grams of fat

1 teaspoon parsley flakes
1 teaspoon basil
1 teaspoon thyme
1 teaspoon oregano
1 teaspoon marjoram

½ teaspoon rosemary
1 teaspoon garlic powder
2 teaspoons onion powder
1 teaspoon salt
1 teaspoon black pepper

1. Combine all ingredients.
2. Store in a tightly covered jar.

Horseradish Sauce

Yields 1 cup   2.5 grams of fat per tablespoon

½ cup Hellmann's Reduced Fat Mayonnaise
½ cup light sour cream

½ teaspoon dry mustard
1 teaspoon lemon juice
2 tablespoons prepared horseradish

1. Combine the ingredients. Store in the refrigerator

House Specialities

Chicken Broth

Chicken and beef broth are important in low-fat cooking; and while canned broths and instant bouillon granules may be used, your own broth will taste better and cost less. You'll find that whole chickens are one of the best buys in your meat counter. Remove and reserve the breast meat before placing the remaining chicken in the soup kettle. After the broth is prepared, freeze or use as a base for soups, casseroles and vegetables.

Yields 5 cups   0 grams of fat per serving

- 1 whole chicken or stewing hen
- 8 cups water
- 1 cup combined chopped celery leaves, green onion tops and parsley
- Chunks of carrots, onions or bits of vegetables you have been saving
- 1 tablespoon lemon juice

1. Remove giblets from inside the cavity of the chicken. Debone the breast portion for later use. Place remaining chicken and giblets, except liver, in a large soup kettle.
2. Add water, vegetable broth and vegetables. Bring to a boil. Reduce the heat and simmer for 1 hour, skimming when necessary.
3. Remove the chicken from the broth, cool enough to handle and pull the meat from the bones. Reserve for later use.
4. Return the bones to the kettle; continue to simmer until broth is reduced by about one-third.
5. Strain broth into a large bowl; refrigerate.
6. Remove fat that rises to the top and solidifies, leaving you fat-free, sodium-free broth to use as needed. Freeze any broth you will not use within 3-4 days.

House Specialties

Yogurt Cheese

Yogurt cheese has the consistency of cream cheese but none of the fat. It can be substituted for cream cheese, sour cream or mayonnaise in many recipes, especially in appetizers or desserts. It is simple to make, but allow about 8 hours for it to drain. It will keep 1-2 weeks in the refrigerator. If you want to use it in cooking, add 1 tablespoon cornstarch for each cup of cheese to prevent it from separating while cooking.

Yields 1 cup   0 grams of fat

2 cups nonfat yogurt that does not contain gelatin or stabilizer

1. Line a strainer with a coffee filter or cheesecloth. Set the strainer over a deep bowl, making sure that the bottom of the strainer is at least an inch from the bottom of the bowl.
2. Spoon the yogurt into the coffee filter; cover with plastic film and refrigerate.
3. Allow yogurt to drain for 8-10 hours or until the cheese reaches the desired consistency. The longer it drains the thicker it will become.

House Specialties

Cream Sauce or Soup Substitute

This recipe gives you an option when you want a fat-free, low-sodium cream base for sauces or soups. You can vary the taste by adding your own seasoning. The dry mix of the base keeps in the refrigerator indefinitely. Mix it with water and heat it when needed.

Yields 1½ cups of dry mix   8 grams of fat total

- 1 cup instant non-fat dry milk
- 1 tablespoon dried onion flakes
- 6 tablespoons cornstarch
- ¼ teaspoon black pepper
- 2 tablespoons instant chicken bouillon (low sodium)
- ½ teaspoon basil, (optional)
- ½ teaspoon thyme, (optional)

1. Combine all of the ingredients and store in a tightly covered container in the refrigerator.
2. When you want to use the base, mix ⅓ cup of the dry base with 1¼ cups of water and stir over low heat until thickened. Celery, broccoli, onions, mushrooms, cheese, etc., may be added as desired.

House Specialities

Special vinegars are a wonderful addition to a good cook's pantry shelf. They can be found in gourmet sections of large grocery stores and specialty cooking shops; or they are simple and inexpensive to make yourself. One of the nicest gifts you can offer a friend or hostess is a bottle of your own special vinegar in an interesting bottle. With a little creative experimentation, you will discover how much the special flavors add to your favorite recipes.

Special Vinegars

HERBAL VINEGAR: Tuck several sprigs of freshly picked herbs (tarragon, basil, rosemary or dill) stem first into 4 or 5 small bottles. Partly crush a few of the herbs to add more flavor. Heat 4 cups of cider or white vinegar in a stainless steel pan until it begins to simmer; do not allow it to boil. Pour the heated vinegar over the herbs in the bottles, seal and let cool. Allow the vinegar to stand for several days for full flavor to develop.

GARLIC AND PEPPER VINEGAR: To add more zip to Herbal Vinegar, combine peeled garlic cloves and fresh hot peppers with the herbs before adding the hot vinegar.

BERRY VINEGAR: In a blender, pureé 1 cup of raspberries, strawberries or blueberries with 2 cups of white vinegar. Pour into a 2-quart bottle; add another 2 cups of vinegar and cover. Allow to mature for 3-4 weeks. Strain into smaller bottles.

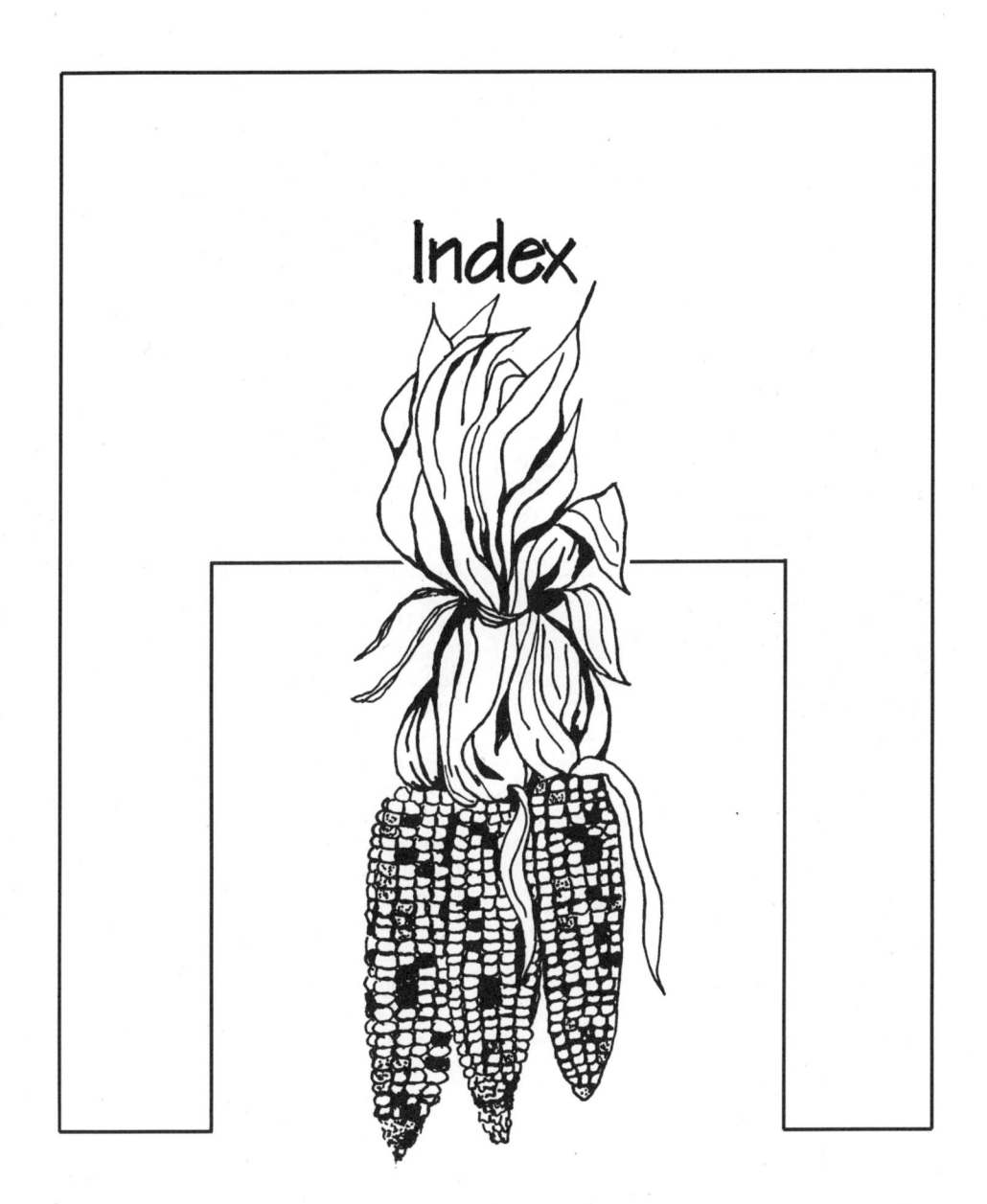

Index

Index

Ames Vegetable Casserole 76
Antipasto, Iowa 9
Appetizers
    Black Bean Dip 3
    Broiled Shrimp 8
    Crab-Stuffed Tomatoes 5
    Iowa Antipasto 9
    Mushroom-Stuffed Shells 7
    Pita Crisps 4
    Skinny Dippers 4
    Spinach-Stuffed Mushrooms 6
    Tortilla Roll-Ups 10
Apple Butter, Stove Top 109
Apple Crisp, Madison County 89
Baked Fish Fillets with Almonds 59
Baked Onions, Creamy 79
Baked Pork Chops, Easy 53
Baked Wild Rice 86
Banana-Nut Bread 20
Bean and Rice Salad 35
Black Bean Dip 3
Black Bean and Corn Salad 33
Beans
    and Rice Salad 35
    Black Bean and Corn Salad 33
    Dip, Black 3
    Five Bean Salad, Okoboji 35
    Jean's 78
Beans, Jean's 78
Beef
    Grilled Kabobs 54
    Heart Smart Meatloaf 57
    Iowa Rib Roast 55
    Meatballs with Noodles,
        Mrs. Martin's 58
    Potter's Swiss Steak 56

Beets, Pickled 110
Best White Bread 14
Bickel's Squirrel Feed for Fifty 65
Black Bean Dip 3
Black Bean and Corn Salad 33
Bobbie's Spinach Salad 31
Breads
    Banana-Nut Bread 20
    Best White Bread 14
    Cornbread, Paradise 13
    Crepes, Whole-Wheat 18
    Dilly Bread 15
    Griddle Cakes, Three-Grain 16
    Pita Crisps 4
    Skinny Dippers 4
Broccoli Bake, Dor's Spinach 77
Broccoli-Tomato Pasta 63
Broiled Shrimp 8
Broiled Parmesan Tomatoes 70
Broth, Chicken 113
Broth, Pesto Tomato 26
Cake
    Chocolate, Laura's 100
    Lemon Glaze 102
Calico Salad 34
Caroline's Pesto 26
Carrots and Zucchini, Matchstick 75
Chicken
    Breast, Pan-Grilled 43
    Breast, Pecan-Crusted 41
    Broth 113
    Fricassee 45
    Flat-Out Garlic 46
    Maytag Blue 42
    Stuffing Casserole 44
Chicken Fricassee 45

Chicken Stuffing Casserole 44
Chocolate
    Banana Bread Pudding 97
    Cake, Laura's 100
    Roll 98
Citrus Salad, Tangy 32
Cookies
    Date Dreams 104
    Date-Nut Bars 103
    Quick No-Bake 105
Corn
    and Black Bean Salad 33
    Chowder, Iowa 23
    Cornbread, Paradise 13
    Easy Corn on the Cob 72
    Grilled, on the Cob 73
Cornish Hens with Fruit 50
Country Potatoes 84
Crab-Stuffed Tomatoes 5
Cranberry-Orange Relish 111
Cream Sauce, Soup Base 115
Creamy Baked Onions 79
Crepes, Whole-Wheat 18
Cucumbers
    Dilled 28
    with Garden Tomatoes 29
Date Dreams 104
Date-Nut Bars 103
Desserts
    Chocolate-Banana Bread
        Pudding 97
    Chocolate Roll 98
    Madison County Apple Crisp 89
    Patty's Frozen Strawberry 92
    Peach-Blueberry Crisp 90
    Strawberry-Rhubarb Crunch 93
    Summer Peach Trifle 91
Dilled Potato Salad, San's 37

Dilly Bread 15
Dor's Broccoli-Spinach Bake 77
Drake U. Slice-O-Lemon Pie 95
Easy-Baked Pork Chops 53
Easy Corn on the Cob 72
Favorite Grilled Kabobs 54
Fish, Baked 59
Five-Bean Salad, Okoboji 35
Flat-Out Garlic Chicken 46
Fried Potatoes, Not-To-Worry 82
Fresh Dilled Cucumbers 28
Game Hens, Cornish with Fruit 50
Garden Gazpacho 27
Garden Ratatouille 69
Garden Tomatoes with Cucumbers 29
Gazpacho, Garden 27
Glazed Lemon Bundt Cake 102
Glazed Turkey Breast 48
Grapefruit Pie 96
Griddle Cakes, Three-Grain 16
Grilled
    Chicken Breast, Pan 43
    Corn on the Cob 73
    Kabobs 54
    Pork Tenderloin 51
    Turkey Breast, State Fair 49
Harvest Pumpkin Pie 94
Heart-Smart Meatloaf 57
Hearty Vegetable Soup 25
Herb Seasoning Mix 112
Horseradish Sauce 112
Iowa
    Antipasto 9
    Corn Chowder 23
    Rib Roast 55
Jean's Beans 78
Jo's New Potato Salad 36
Lasagna, White 64

Laura's Chocolate Cake 100
Lemon Bundt Cake, Glazed 102
Lemon Pie, Drake U. Slice-O- 95
Low-Fat Scalloped Potatoes 80
Madison County Apple Crisp 89
Marv's Seafood Pasta 60
Matchstick Zucchini and Carrots 75
Maytag Blue, Chicken 42
Meatballs, Mrs. Martin's 58
Meatloaf, Heart-Smart 57
Medallions of Pork Tenderloin 32
Microwave Pecan Brittle 106
Mrs. Martin's Meatballs with Noodles ...58
Mushroom-Stuffed Shells 7
Mushrooms, Spinach-Stuffed 6
New Chicken Fricassee 45
New Potatoes with Mushrooms 80
Not-to-Worry Fried Potatoes 85
Okoboji Five-Bean Salad 35
Onions, Creamy Baked 79
Orange, Cranberry Relish 111
Oven-Roasted Sliced Potatoes 81
Pan-Grilled chicken Breast 43
Paradise Cornbread 13
Pasta with Broccoli-Tomato Sauce 63
Patty's Frozen Strawberry 92
Peach-Blueberry Crisp 90
Peach Trifle, Summer 91
Pecan Brittle, Microwave 106
Pecan Chicken Breasts 42
Pesto, Caroline's 26
Pesto Tomato Broth 26
Pickled Beets 110
Pickled Peaches 110
Pie
    Drake U. Slice-o-Lemon 95
    Grapefruit Pie 96
    Harvest Pumpkin 94

Pita Crisps 4
Pork Chops, Easy-Baked 53
    Grilled Tenderloin 51
    Medallions with Peppers 52
Potato Soup with Green Chilies 24
Potatoes
    Country 84
    Dilled Potato Salad, San's 37
    Jo's New Potato Salad 36
    New, with Mushrooms 80
    Not-to-Worry Fried 82
    Oven-Roasted, Sliced 81
    Roasted Root Vegetables 85
    Scalloped, Low-Fat 80
    Soup with Green Chilies 24
    Stuffed Baked 83
Potter's Swiss Steak 56
Pumpkin Pie, Harvest 94
Quick No-Bake Cookies 105
Ratatouille, Garden 69
Rhubarb-Strawberry Crunch 93
Rice and Bean Salad 35
Roasted Root Vegetables 85
Salads
    Bobbie's Spinach 31
    Calico 34
    Corn and Black Bean 33
    Five-Bean, Okoboji 35
    Fresh Dilled Cucumber 28
    Garden Tomatoes with
        Cucumbers 29
    Jo's New Potato 36
    Rice and Bean 35
    San's Dilled Potato 37
    Strawberry-Spinach 30
    Tangy Citrus 32
San's Dilled Potato Salad 37
Sauteed Scallops with Vegetables 61

Scalloped Potatoes, Low-Fat 80
Scallops, Sauteed with Vegetables 61
Seafood Pasta, Marv's 60
Seasoning Mix, Herb 112
Shrimp, Broiled 8
Skinny Dippers 4
Sliced Oven-Roasted Potatoes 81
Soups
    Garden Gazpacho 27
    Hearty Vegetable 25
    Iowa Corn Chowder 23
    Pesto Tomato Broth 26
    Potato Soup Creen Chilies 24
Special Vinegars 116
Spinach-Stuffed Mushrooms 6
Spinach
    Broccoli Bake, Dor's 77
    Salad, Bobbie's 31
    Strawberry-Spinach Salad 30
    Stuffed Mushrooms 6
    Wapsipinicon Tomatoes 71
Squirrel Feed for Fifty, Bickel's 65
State Fair Grilled Turkey Tenderloins 49
Strawberry Frozen Dessert 92
Strawberry-Rhubarb Crunch 93
Strawberry-Spinach Salad 30
Stove Top Apple Butter 109
Stuffed Baked Potato 83
Stuffed Cherry Tomatoes, Crab 5
Stuffed Mushrooms, Spinach 6
Stuffed Mushroom Shells 7
Summer Peach Trifle 91
Swiss Steak, Potter's 56
Tangy Citrus Salad 32
Three-Grain Griddle Cakes 16
Tomatoes
    Broiled Parmesan 70
    Crab-Stuffed Cherry 5

    Garden, with Cucumbers 29
    Pasta with, Broccoli Sauce 63
    Pesto Broth 26
    Tuna Pita Pockets 62
    Wapsipinicon 71
Tortilla Roll-Ups 10
Trifle, Summer Peach 91
Tuna-Tomato Pita Pockets 62
Turkey
    Cutlets with Lemon Sauce 47
    Glazed Breast 48
    Tenderloins, State Fair Grilled 49
Turkey Cutlets with Lemon Sauce 47
Vegetable Casserole, Ames 76
Vegetable Medley 74
Vegetables. (Also see specific types)
    Hearty Soup 25
    Roasted Root 85
    Scallops, Sautéed with 61
    Casserole, Ames 76
    Medley 74
Vinegar, Special 116
Wapsipinicon Tomatoes 71
White Lasagna 64
Whole-Wheat Crepes 18
Wild Rice, Baked 86
Yogurt Cheese 114
Zucchini, and Carrots 75

CONTRIBUTORS

San Anderson	Clinton
Jeanette Baker	Paradise Valley
John Bickel	McGregor
Miriam Erickson Brown	Des Moines
Lois Clark	Burlington
Phyllis Conrad	Cedar Rapids
Patty Crispin	Tingley
Jo Freeman	Des Moines
Karen Green	Castalia
Lois Klein	Des Moines
Betty Koch	Des Moines
Caroline Levine	Des Moines
Sue Lovall	Waterloo
Marlys Potter	Nevada
Mary Siberell	Des Moines
Dorothea Sidney	Des Moines
Jo Sloan	Des Moines
Jim Stevens	Newton
Edna Tegtmeier	Ames
Helen Westcot	Cedar Rapids

OUR SPECIAL THANKS TO:

Anderson Erickson Dairy for permission to reprint their White Lasagne recipe from one of their brochures.

Green's Sugarbush Farm for permission to depict their farm in an illustration.

Maytag Dairy Farms for permission to use their recipe for Chicken Maytag Blue.

Jean Durkee for allowing the recipe for Vegetable Medley to be reprinted from her book *Tout de Suite à la Microwave*.

NOTES

NOTES

NOTES

NOTES

About Peg Hein and Kathryn Lewis

Recipes from Iowa....with Love, published in 1981, was the first book Peg did in collaboration with Kathryn. The two have since worked together on four other books and have been pleased and amazed at their success and reception. ***New Tastes of Iowa*** brings the mother-daughter team back to their Iowa roots.

Peg, a Des Moines wife, mother and recipe collector for thirty-five years, was involved in community, church and professional activities before she and her husband Marv moved to Austin, Texas. Love of Iowa and Iowa friends and family continued to reinforce her Iowa connection.

Kathryn was born in Davenport, grew up in Des Moines and spent several years in Burlington as a young wife and mother. She designs and produces gift items that are sold throughout Iowa and the rest of the United States. She now lives in Austin with her husband, Peter, and two children, Nick and Laura.

New Tastes of Iowa

To order additional copies of *New Tastes of Iowa,* use the order blanks provided below.

Kathryn Designs
2215-A Westlake Drive
Austin, Texas 78746

Please send _____ copies of *New Tastes of Iowa* to:

Name _____

Address _____

City _____ State _____ Zip Code _____

Enclosed is $8.50 plus $2.25 for postage and handling.

— —

New Tastes of Iowa

To order additional copies of *New Tastes of Iowa,* use the order blanks provided below.

Kathryn Designs
2215-A Westlake Drive
Austin, Texas 78746

Please send _____ copies of *New Tastes of Iowa* to:

Name _____

Address _____

City _____ State _____ Zip Code _____

Enclosed is $8.50 plus $2.25 for postage and handling.